This book is dedicated to
T.E. Lawrence

Thanks – and other things . . .

Thanks for help and/or inspiration to 'Jim Morrison', Veg & Zar, Pete Boyle, Andy Pollard, Bob & Co at the Club, Ben & Laurence, Andy Mitten and all the contributors within – Jamie Smith, Brownie, Jason Davies, Philip Ellis, Ozzie Pete and the brilliant 'Drastic'.

Also, *mega* thanks go to Sara Attwood-Jones (typing, editorial comment etc), Eleanor (who was so good) and Emma (typing) for all their hard work and dedication to the Red cause.

About the Author . . .

Pseudonymous RICHARD KURT is 26 and can be found chain-smoking in the East Stand Lower. He was educated at Manchester Grammar, Manchester University and Manchester United. Before the publication of this first book, he was a history teacher, a member of minor pop groups and a frequent writer for *Red Issue* under the moniker "Red-Eye". Exiled from his Urmston homeland, he currently lives alarmingly near Loonypool with his girl, a guitar and a hamster called Mickey Phelan.

About the Future . . .

UNITED WE STOOD: THE RED ARMY YEARS is the companion to this book and is planned for spring 1995. We would like this to be fan-based and therefore invite Reds to write in about their most memorable moments from the years 1974-1986 – from relegation to the end of Big Ron. We're particularly interested in stories and opinions about 'terrace events'; the great Stretford End of the '70s; fan fashions; the awaydays; the ICJ and trips to Europe, as well as the great on-pitch occasions.

Please write to the author c/o Sigma Press.

UNITED WE STOOD

THE UNOFFICIAL HISTORY OF
THE FERGUSON YEARS

RICHARD KURT

Published by Sigma Leisure - an imprint of
Sigma Press, 1 South Oak Lane, Wilmslow, Cheshire SK9 6AR,
England.

Reprinted: 1995, 1996.

British Library Cataloguing in Publication Data
A CIP record for this book is available from the British Library.

ISBN: 1-85058-432-X

Typesetting and Design: Sigma Press, Wilmslow, Cheshire.

Cover photo: Martin

Flag & Design: Loz

Cover design : Martin Mills

Illustrations: courtesy of/copyright Red Issue & Loz except for
the cartoon on page 135, which is by I. Bailey; all other
illustrations are by *Red Issue* artists and Loz of Parby Reds.

Printed by: MFP Design & Print, 0161 864 4540.

CONTENTS

1986-87

Nobody looks forward to a game at Southampton. 'The Dell' is, of course, the Old English for 'the pit' or alternatively 'bog-standard Endsleigh-style hovel'. It takes a week to travel there, the beer is offensively bad and the police take a special country bumpkin delight in annoying Northern urbanites. Thanks to the failure of the team to beat the Saints at home in the League cup tie at the end of October – a midweek nil-nil of almost unparalleled awfulness – we now had to trek down there the following Tuesday for an unwanted replay. How Ron must have wished that the lads had sealed the tie at the first attempt: we lost 4-1, it could have been six or seven and within 36 hours, Atkinson was history.

Funnily enough, until Southampton scored just before half-time, it seemed United could win it. Ever the optimists, we could convince ourselves that Saturday's appalling draw against Coventry – after which well chosen epithets were bellowed at the box, bench and anyone else in range – was the nadir from which we could now rise in triumph. A nice little Cup run would do the trick; the confidence would flood back and the team return to the glories of 12 months ago. Ha. There's nothing as blind as the devotion of the Red.

In a horrific second half, Scouse reject Jimmy Case ran roughshod through our utterly inept midfield. It was truly horrible, like watching Scotland in the World Cup or City last season. Skulking back to Manchester, counting the lost wages of an afternoon off work, you couldn't help but feel that there would be no end to this nightmare without some sort of drastic action from someone. In the event, it was to be Martin Edwards

1

who took the plunge, much to Ron's evident surprise and, perhaps, to the relief of most of us.

It had all looked so different only seven weeks before. True, we'd been bottom of the table at the end of August after a hugely embarrassing home defeat by Charlton but it could be argued that this was all a post-World Cup hangover and the result of yet another mini-injury crisis; the perennial cry of the '80s United fan was sounded – 'wait till Robbo gets back.' And when he did come back, ironically against our nemesis Southampton, we won rampagingly 5-1 in a manner reminiscent of earlier Atkinson sides.

Sadly, this match turned out to be the last hurrah of an obsolescent 11. The performance was that of an ageing tart, slapping on the make-up and suspenders for one last glorious display before she disappears off the streets forever. After that day, there was little to savour but a decentish win over Wednesday and yet another Stapleton derby goal. The team looked tired, old, dispirited and totally lacking in motivation. By the time of the night of infamy at the Dell, United were four places off rock bottom with three league wins in three months. No one needed reminding that a year before, we'd been top of the league by a mile. What had gone wrong?

Of course, looking back now, the announcement of Hughesy's forthcoming departure in the New Year takes on a symbolic importance. We all know what happened to his personal form after that and how it affected the team as a whole. The fact that local hospitals were filling up with United casualties cannot be ignored, however much of an 'excuse' it seems to be. But above these physical realities, you sensed something else, something wrong in the spirit of the Club.

For the first time in years, it appeared that many fans started out in '86/'87 *knowing* that we could not win the League, a shocking contrast to our usual feverish optimism. Ron Atkinson seemed to feel the same; he considered quitting throughout the summer and always suspected that '86/'87 would be make or break time. There was an air of desperation about our failure

2

to clinch the title when all the indications seemed so favourable – now that the omens looked less delightful, how could we hope to win it?

Atkinson's transfer policy, always a topic for animated discussion at the best of times, increasingly appeared to reflect this desperation. In fact, if you're looking for a quick answer as to why Ron failed, check out his last five major purchases: the two Gibsons, Barnes, Davenport and Sivebaek for an outlay of almost £2 million, roughly what we got for Hughes. What a dazzling array of talent! How they are lovingly remembered by the faithful! What a testament to Ron's market judgement! Add the talent and contributions of all five together and it wouldn't approach what Hughes could give in one month. No doubt the Board must have come to a similar conclusion – a transfer deficit of £1.5 million in total and nothing to show for it but a bottom-of-the-table team. Crucially, gates were down too.

Ron himself has argued that if he'd been allowed to buy Terry Butcher after the World Cup, it could've made all the difference; he felt the need for a new partner for McGrath. It's a puzzling point; even in those first months of '86/'87, United only conceded more than one goal a game twice in 16 matches – it was going *forward* that was the problem. Clearly, he was right to be unhappy that the Board simply refused him permission to buy Butcher although in this particular case, you feel we had a lucky escape...

So much for first impressions. Perhaps the key to Atkinson's departure is not so much in the surface stuff but in the background noise. As players have come forward gradually with their versions of those troubled times, it becomes apparent that United as a club was beginning to resemble Big Ron in too many ways. The caricature of Ron that he was happy to let circulate was of a larger-than-life, flashy, bejewelled, all-year tanned, mouthy Scouse wideboy-made-good.

Confronted with such a creature, you immediately suspect that there's less to him than meets the eye. Whilst he may well be capable of pulling off grandiose achievements and cunning

3

stunts that capture the eye and imagination, fundamentally he is incapable of reaching the truly Olympian heights of title wins and Euro success because such triumphs require more than just surface glitter. They demand rigorous rebuilding, constant and consistent application, persistently good judgement and professionalism in relations with underlings.

From '81 to '86, United were the on-pitch manifestations of Ron's character; ebullient, entertaining, passionate, intelligent yet also maddeningly inconsistent, prone to sloppiness, over-confidence and simply 'winging it.' Moreover, the Club as a whole was later revealed to be suffering from 'Atkinson's Disease' – whilst everything on the visible surface, i.e. the first team, was swish and glam and tanned, underneath the foundations were rotting away from neglect. When the tan fades and the jewellery gets hocked as in the autumn of '86, the pallid flabby carcass is exposed to the world. When Ferguson arrived, he found a club whose youth and reserve teams were in disarray, a scouting system suffering advanced senile dementia and an atmosphere soaked in alcohol fumes and ill-feeling.

Of course, Ron's caricature was just that – a wildly exaggerated image. Kevin Moran talks of a man who was actually quite shy and modest underneath; Lou Macari has pointed out that he was actually no great drinker who'd only take one sipped glass from a bottle of bubbly. Much of this 'Malcolm Allison' myth-making was simply a construct for a media who wanted this act from him and, perhaps, he in turn was keen to contrast himself with his predecessor who had been seen as too boring and reserved. Nevertheless, you feel compelled to conclude that Ron was a man in a hurry, desperate to buy a team to win a title with little thought of dynastic ambition or long-term planning for the club as a whole. And who can blame him? The implicit job description – win a title in five years or get the sack – must have impelled him to take such a course.

The nub of the matter isn't then his failure to build a champion *club* but his failure to produce a champion *team*. There has to be a suspicion that he was never the man to do

4

even that. In a long, varied, often glorious, usually exciting career, Atkinson has never produced a champion side. His best Villa and West Brom sides who promised so much tended to fold in just the way that his United teams did; they have all tended to lack the single-mindedness, the discipline, the stamina or the steel to go all the way over nine months.

Wilkins, Coppell, Robbo and others all attest to the truth that Atkinson is one of the greatest motivators of teams in football. In the big one-off confrontation, especially when the underdog, there's no better man to have at the helm. Focused on the single match, the final, the crucial title summit game, he has always excelled himself. All his sides were capable of beating anyone on their day. He seems to have the gift of picking the right game-plan, team and words for these occasions – we all know how he did this for United and also against us at Wembley and elsewhere since. But in a campaign situation, filled with the run-of-the-mill games and requiring a long-term perspective and mentality, he seems to be lacking. Perhaps he was always destined to bring us Wembley glories and famous victories over the Scouse but never the title.

Little of the above featured in the press coverage of Ron's travails during '86 – indeed, the consensus soon formed that he had been unlucky and certainly hadn't been given enough time to win the title. Sadly, one suspects that Ron wouldn't have won a title at United if he'd been given a century. Instead, the media spotlight played gleefully upon an emerging 'discipline problem' and the way Ron related to the lads. The papers had discovered the Man United Drinking Club – old news to anyone in Manc who knew of players who were counted as 'regulars' in at least a dozen city centre beer emporiums.

Poor Hughesy, self-christened 'Old Lager Legs', had spent the last six months of his Manchester life getting increasingly bladdered around town; stories began to circulate about other older players being sighted in various states of wreckage and later Arnold Muhren was vividly to describe in his book the stench of stale beer breath every morning at training as the liggers staggered into Old Trafford. The scene surfaced publicly in the summer when half a dozen players were fined for inappropriate drinking on a tour of Holland. It was hard to avoid making a linkage between United's collapse in '86 and this apparent bar-room culture at the club – and Alex Ferguson was not slow to make his opinion felt when he arrived.

Worse was to follow. Tales of dressing room tiffs and poor morale did the rounds; combined with the drinking stories, a damning picture of a team out of control and engaged in early-'70s style factionalism was being happily painted by the press. Then, in October, during a training session Olsen went in to tackle Remi Moses. Moses, perhaps unstrung by the shock of witnessing Olsen tackle anyone, reacted by belting the frail Dane in the face. Jesper came off, streaming blood from an eye-socket wound, in sight of two astonished hacks. Atkinson told the press that it had been a freak training accident, which didn't help – the world lapped up this all-too-public confirmation of United's internal strife. Tellingly, Robbo doesn't deny in his book that this incident was typical of the time. The vision of United in '86 was not a pretty one – a bunch of ageing pissheads lumbering around muttering "Are you startin'?"

Clearly, Ron was no fire-and-brimstone disciplinarian in the Fergie Fury mould and in some ways this was a strength; a team of talented wilful individuals could only have played with the carefree, exuberant abandon so often displayed in those years if the manager treats them in the libertarian, indulgent way that Ron seemed to favour. There's nothing wrong in that per se – it's more a question of getting the balance right between allowing free expression and maintaining collective cohesion. Much to our surprise, it has turned out that Fergie has achieved this balance whereas it appears Ron did not.

Bryan Robson, perhaps the best possible witness as a man who clearly loved Ron, says as much in his books; Ron, a lover of dressing room camaraderie who became a close friend to many players, was too prepared to be lenient with his boys. He

6

hadn't maintained enough of a distance – he was virtually one of the lads. Instead of maintaining a teacher-pupil relationship, he'd become more like a prefect to the boys. When trouble brewed, he wasn't in the best position to lower the temperature from a position of true authority, according to some observers.

Moreover, whilst he was able to count on the absolute loyalty of his 'friends' in the team, others resented what they saw as his egotistical manner and unyielding dogmatism. Finally – and crucially – when matters went awry on the pitch, some players looked to Ron for the managerial magic sponge and were disappointed with what they got. Frank Stapleton, admittedly a notorious whinger, said that Ron didn't seem to be able to give the team that little something to get them out of the rut, as if he expected it just to happen merely because the players were so experienced. For Ron, it was a tragic dualism that the facets of his style that guaranteed we reached the heights during the good times also worked against us in the darker moments.

Despite all the factors working against him in November '86, perhaps Ron might have survived if he could have added to the partial support from the players the whole-hearted support of the fans. Had he been as loved as the Doc, surely Edwards would not have dared to sack him? For the fact remains that Ron's record was good. Two Cups, a whisker away from a Euro final, good crowds and not one duff season – he never finished out of the top four. To put it in perspective, only once in Fergie's first five years did United finish higher than we did in Ron's *worst* seasons. Sure, United with Ron would have probably finished poorly in '86/'87 but he could probably have patched things up enough to 'do well' the year after.

Nevertheless, however loved Ron's teams and their football were by us, Ron personally was never really taken to our bosom. Perhaps we should have appreciated the real man under the image but were blinded by the glare of his flash. Whatever the reason, whether because he was a Scouser or a Flash Harry or just a fat rich git wearing too much gold, we treated him with some respect and a lot of suspicion. It seems cruel that we have cherished his teams, his ideals, the memories he helped create without cherishing *him* but that's curmudgeonly Reds for you. When the call to save Ron came, we certainly weren't going to be there to help him, not after that crap Coventry game anyway. For a few years afterwards, many of us were to regret our decision, for Alex Ferguson certainly didn't bring instant remedies with him down from Scotland – in fact, we were often to question whether he'd brought anything with him except an ability to turn all he touched to shit.

* * * * *

RED-EYE

"It is a matter of opinion whether or not the present side is better than Sir Matt Busby's. It is a matter of fact that they are certainly the best since 1967. It would be wrong, though, to say that the quarter of a century between the two was packed with non-descript football and faceless players. Each era, each season threw up its own ups and downs and crowd favourites, each appealing to a different section of the Red Army. There are still the Busby purists, die-hard members of the Doc's Red Army (winged denim jacket compulsory) and even masochists who get off on Dave Sexton. But for me, the United side of the early-to-mid eighties holds some special memories.

As any drug user will tell you, the first hit is always the best, after which you are constantly chasing that initial buzz – football is no exception. Between the ages of 7 and 12, I was one of the day-tripper brigade. Trips to Old Trafford were restricted to birthdays and special occasions and always with a parent in tow. (My auntie took me against Leeds in 1979 and nearly had a coronary but that's another story). It was only after I started secondary school in 1983 that I was allowed to go with my friends and stand on the Stretford End.

What I experienced that day had a major effect on the rest of my life. I was hooked instantly. The crowd's reaction to United's goal left me with a ringing in my ears that didn't subside till long after the final whistle. The good-natured pushing and shoving, the banter with the players, the songs.

8

Half-time: the ropy cheeseburgers and piss-weak tea, the people pissing wherever there was a free space on the wall. Second Half: more of the same and returning home on the GM Buses Football Special which seemed to house more singers than the whole of the West Stand. All this had a profound impact on a young, impressionable 12-year-old lad.

There's nothing extraordinary about the above, it's been experienced by thousands of football fans, not just those of United. But it happened to me during the Atkinson era and that's what makes it so special.

United won every home game in style, there were 55,000 at every home game, all wearing ski hats even though the game was played in scorching heat and "Tarzan Boy" was played at least 10 times before each game. It wasn't really like that but that's how I like to remember it."

Jamie Smith, Little Hulton

*   *   *   *   *

Alex Ferguson came to United wearing the mantle of the best manager in the Scottish League, although that's not saying much is it? A bit like proclaiming Joe Royle top boss in Oldham really. Still, he'd broken the Glaswegian duopoly and had triumphed in Europe; United fans remembered his Aberdeen side from a Euro tie as being a useful outfit who'd given us two excellent contests. His background had reassuringly Busbyesque overtones and at least in matters of discipline, it seemed the team would be in for a collective colonic irrigation, so to speak; he was determined to flush out the traces of alcohol and eliminate those saggy muscles and growing paunches that had become *de rigeur*.

It would be too easy to over-dramatise the contrast with Ron – which is precisely why the press did just that – and imagine Fergie sneaking round OT armed with a breathalyser and sharpened cups 'n' saucers to hurl at recidivist players but the change in regime was tangible. Basically, Fergie was one of that dreaded breed, Blazer Man; smart haircuts, proper attire, sober habits and attention to public image were now the order of the day. A Scottish Oliver Cromwell had brought Puritanism to the decadent remnants of the old king's court and many weren't particularly happy about it. Alex, clued up on OT customs by Muhren's book and Strachan's phone calls, wasted little time in imposing his new Code of Conduct which included an end to the popular but debilitating lunchtime drinking binges. A hundred publicans wept but fitness and performance on the pitch noticeably improved. Wisely, Alex had assured everybody from the outset that no judgements had been made – it was up to the players to prove they deserved to stay. Over the three winter months, United lost only one League match which just goes to show how complacent they'd been in Ron's last days.

Oblique references in Fergie's and Robbo's later comments clearly demonstrated that there was some on-going resistance to the new regime in the dressing room for months afterwards. You can make an educated guess as to who were the 'several' players who resented Ron's dismissal. Footballers are often simple creatures who offer devotion in the same way a puppy does; feed it well and it loves you forever – kick it in the head for pissing on your programme collection and it never forgives you. Fergie talks of having to get rid of older and injury-prone players at the time but surely there must have been an element of 'cleansing' in this process.

He was in the position of an Allied general having to engage in post-war deNazification; to create a loyal support, you have to risk losing talented people. He was later to sell players who still had much to offer – but not to a Fergusonised United. Alex would explain that certain players had to go not because he personally couldn't work with them but because they were incompatible with the new ideology of the Club. It's a clever point – the *causus belli* was not Alex but 'Fergusonism', the ideal which the Board had decided to impose and which was bigger than any individual. It's a theme that runs right through Alex's 'Six Years at United' but didn't find much favour with Whiteside fans 18 months later . . .

For the next six months, however, a state of grace existed

between the Roundheads and the Cavaliers, punctured by two unfortunate indicators of what was to come. In March '87, Strachan, Garton, McGrath and Moran were all publicly fined for the heinous crime against humanity of missing a team bus; in May, Norm and McGrath, rapidly gaining a reputation of Ollie Reed proportions, were fined for drink abuse on tour in Malta. Clearly, the Era of Prohibition was going to be harder for some than others.

* * * * *

On the pitch, after a dire start to Alex's reign in which United scored only once in four games, the effect of playing for one's future soon kicked in. In the context of such an excremental season, December and January qualified as golden months. Two six-goal thrillers against Spurs and Villa, despite the fact that we lost two-goal leads in both, raised the spirits a little, particularly as Davenport bagged two doubles including one scored from a Giggsian acute angle. Whiteside had come back from injury to go up front and scored on his return; amazingly enough, Colin Gibson did the same against Leicester. Six days later, we faced a Boxing Day outing to Anfield – remarkably, seven years to the day since we'd last lost a League game there.

As usual, the Mickeys were frothing at the mouth in rabid anticipation, no doubt having convinced themselves that the Old Trafford turmoil would prove to be the decisive factor in their favour. There's no shame in admitting that many Reds heading for the Liverpool slums did so with some trepidation, not so much for fear of the beating the Double-holders might inflict on us but in memory of February's delightful reception offered to the team by the lovable Scousers. There had since been a huge PR exercise by the two clubs to foster good feeling (!) involving on-coach fraternisation and plans for joint supporters' functions but we all suspected that this was more a case of an outbreak of "Scouse Media Awareness Complex(S.M.A.C.)" in the Anfield boardroom than any genuine contrition.

11

Sure enough, taking our places in the murderers' breeding ground, we caught sight of an unmissable cut-out of a 747 with 'Munich 58' scrawled upon it. How gratified we were to know that Loonypool were keeping faith with their traditions. The usual Munich songs and coin-throwing contests duly followed. As is also traditional, of course, we outfought the so-called champions and won with a Stapleton goal, silencing the gibbering hordes on the Kop and duly recording what turned out to be our only away win of the League programme. How completely perfect: even in the midst of the worst season for travelling Reds in living memory, we still managed to do the Dirties. In fact, Liverpool were to end the season trophy-free – and as it turned out, our two games with them were to turn out to prove vital factors in their failure. The legend of the Scousebusters lives.

During a fab fortnight in January, which we'd kicked off with the fourth tonking of the Toons we'd enjoyed since they got promoted, Big Norm stamped his weight heavily upon the Bitters and the Gooners. City, let us happily remind ourselves, were streaking towards their habitual '80s home of Division Two with the worst ever attack seen in Manchester – 36 goals in 42 games. Drawing us at OT was their highlight of the year and they came blatantly for a 0-0; in front of 54,700, Norm extinguished their last hopes of any sort of glory.

Two weeks later, pace-setters Arsenal arrived at OT unbeaten in 22 games and looking to repeat their Xmas '85 result. Within minutes, Norm had wrapped his legs around O'Leary's neck, promptly causing Arsenal to lose their heads. A frenzied ruckus took place – Arsenal do love a good brawl don't they? – and from that moment on they were always second best, two lateish goals sealing it for the Reds after Rocastle's assault on Norm got the red card. Arsenal didn't win another game till April after that, thus blowing the title completely. The Cockney Reds went home cock-a-hoop.

This Indian Summer of a winter came to an end with a home Cup defeat by Coventry in which United were basically beaten by perhaps the worst match-pitch of the decade. They might as well have played the game at Altrincham ice-rink. Coventry did at least go on to win the Cup against those smug sods at Spurs who'd previously thought every Cup Final was theirs by divine right. The pitch problems at this point were largely caused by the worst undersoil heating system ever installed. Whoever put the damn thing in should have been invoiced for the loss of income our Cup KO had cost. It got replaced in the summer but that wasn't to be the end of our problems with grass (no Lee Sharpe joke intended).

The last three months of the season were eminently forgettable. There was nothing to play for; Fergie was taking the opportunity to test out the squad and ended up using 24 players that season. Crowds slipped down to 32,000; the United Road boys went quiet and the Strettie went back to its books. It felt just like the end of 88/89 – a surprise Cup KO followed by a gentle drift towards summer slumber. We did, of course, rouse ourselves for the visits of the Blues and the Dirties, 54,000 turning up for the latter clash. We were glad to be able to extend a helping hand to our Bitter neighbours, that is by shoving their heads firmly down towards the pit of relegation by beating them 2-0. Robbo scored a supremely sweet goal, finishing off a well-worked move with a crisp drive right under the noses of the traumatised Moss Siders stuffed into the Paddock. As we streamed out, we regaled them with cheerful chants of 'Cheerio, Cheerio' – for which we were to pay heavily next time we met. Still, for two more seasons, Division One would remain blissfully Blue-free as the Bittermen trudged around to such illustrious arenas as Shrewsbury and Hull, clutching their pathetic bananas.

As for the hovel-dwellers, their visit to OT was even more crucial to them than usual; at this point they were still doggedly pursuing the Goodison Klansmen at the top and were indeed due to play them next. Defeat at OT would devastate their league ambitions; what greater incentive did we need? Just to rub it in a little further, we were in the middle of our worst run of the season which was to amount to only one win in seven and which contained the 0-4 humiliation at Spurs – by some distance our most abject display of the year. And yet despite our faecal form and Liverpool's desperation for the points, we won 1-0. How ironic that in the 20-year period since our promotion, it was in this, our worst season, that we did our only League double over Liverpool. How sweet that these victories should have played such a part in wrecking their title ambitions. It was some consolation for us in what had been an otherwise grim 10 months. Incidentally the goalscorer that day was Peter Davenport...

* * * * *

"O tempora, O mores, O Davenport you useless sod" as Horace might have said. Peter Davenport is already fading from the memory despite having an Old Trafford career that spanned four seasons in which he was even the top scorer in '86/'87. His timing on the pitch was always a subject for hot debate but his timing in life was unquestionably awful, though not his fault. He arrived towards the end of the traumatic '85/'86 season when United had already tossed aside the massive advantage accrued from our record-threatening start and was supposed to be the substitute for the departing Hughes. Hardly an enviable role to play; a little like having to go on stage after Jimi Hendrix.

At his best during the crisis-ridden '86/'87 campaign, we were too immersed in the muddy misery of that sad season to give him any credit – indeed, if anything he was so closely identified with that 18 months of collapse and catastrophe that he'd have been better off spending the year in hospital. Fergie, it seemed, took one look at him and promptly began to conspire to sign McClair and bring Hughesy back from exile. Somehow we got Boro to cough up £700,000 for him after a season in which he'd only scored six in 40 games and that was that. Illustrious he was not.

Frankly, it was all very strange. None of us could get very

emotional about him. He was the kid in class you never played with; Maggie would have said he was not "one of us". There was something about the way he played that simply gnawed at your mammaries, that made you feel he was never going to become Red to the core. He was too laid back, too cool, too cerebral – he made it too easy for us to think he wasn't a 110% blood-sweating, bone-smashing, heart-thumping Red. Robbo pleaded in his book that the poor guy couldn't help it but the truth is we were all pining for Hughesy; subconsciously he would be found wanting. Who wouldn't be? You ask a mortal to fill the boots of a demi-god?

Of course, now we realise that greater forces of darkness were at work – the Curse of Cloughie, the vengeance of the tree people. Essentially it worked thus: Clough would pick some likely lad from obscurity, turn him into star, sell him to United for a gargantuan fee at the height of his form whereupon the hapless player would almost immediately become fat, crap, or both. Months of wasted wages and points later, United would be forced to off-load the failure at a violently reduced fee whilst the rest of the nation split its sides guffawing at our ineptitude.

With Gary Birtles, Clough excelled himself when he had the cheek to take the Bearded Blunderer back to the City Ground and was rewarded by the player's prompt return to form. Those were times made for paranoia; I actually believed for several weeks after the resale that Birtles had been sent as some sort of agent to destroy us from within. What else could explain his performances which made him seem like the gleaming new toy that breaks down on Christmas morning?

Therefore, when Neil Webb arrived amidst a swirl of rave reviews I immediately prepared for disaster but this time the Curse worked in a far more insidious way. There was to be no drastic decline, just a steady draining away like some sort of Chinese water torture. We were given flashes of brilliance, sporadic passes of beauty that found long-range targets with Cruise-like precision, all too often cruelly punctuated by injury and an expanding waistline. Belatedly we realised, as his wife sniped at Fergie on TV and injuries miraculously cleared up in time for England games, that the Tricky Trees had pulled yet another fast one. We took our meagre consolation in watching Forest go down. And we pray to every deity available to us that Roy Keane is spared the fate of his forebears. We trust that his Haircut Disaster of '93 is not a harbinger of doom.

* * * * *

DAILY SPURT
Sportdesk

KEANO' IN BARBERSHOP BUTCHERY SHOCK

'It's not what I asked for'

fumes raging Red

SCISSORS

HORROR

SLAPHEAD

THE OMEN

Inside Tonight
Loads on the Reds
More on hair crisis
United pic special
oh, and Franny Lee
buys small club...

Off the pitch, these were slightly strange days. Between the twin disasters of Heysel and Hillsborough, before the fanzine movement truly took off and before Madchester's vibes spread across Britain, terrace culture was stuck in no man's land. There was certainly a sense that aggro in its organised pre-'85 form was now becoming *passé*; arrest and ejection rates at most grounds had plummeted whilst visits to erstwhile centres of hostility became markedly less tense. The police were much better equipped to understand and deal with violence and the European ban dominated the discourse of the time – how could we get back onto the Continent as soon as possible?

A great deal of self-restraint was going on throughout Britain; we knew that any violent incident would be exaggerated, examined minutely and reported to UEFA whose President, Jaques George, was still deeply unsympathetic to our case. Everyone was missing those Euro way trips; no one wanted to be the fans who wrecked our chances of a speedy return although Leeds, Liverpool and Chelsea fans continued to give the opposite impression. Furthermore, there was the fear that any more serious trouble would bring forward action from the Thatcher Government, notorious for their lack of comprehension of football issues. Talk of Euro blacklists, confiscated passports and forced membership cards was well founded, if Thatcher's pronouncements were to be taken seriously. All these factors, painted in against a backdrop of scenes from the Heysel hell, served to militate against any further large-scale aggro, even if the underlying desire for violence had not yet been fully extinguished.

United had made the pre-season tabloid headlines when a Sealink ferry travelling from Harwich to the Hook of Holland had to turn back for Britain two and a half hours into the voyage; United and West Ham fans were on board engaged in a full pitch scrap, using all the implements on a ship that come to hand. The fans were all on the way to watch friendlies(!); 14 arrests and four hospitalisations resulted. It was hardly the Battle of Agincourt and there were plenty of 'civilians' on board who had no idea that such a fight was occuring but the press made the most of it. Buried in the stories was the true cause – Sealink had ignored their own guidelines and police advice and allowed fans on board. They didn't even realise that there were *rival* fans on the ship! With no police around and no segregation, it was hardly surprising that the 30 or so 'well-dressed, older' Hammers (i.e. ICF?) hastened to welcome their Northern friends with a hail of missiles. It turned out that

United outnumbered them three-to-one and thus proceeded to emphasise physically this superiority. . .

In September, the sheep molesting rabble from Leeds took their swastikas to Bradford and gave a demonstration of what the press should really be concerned about. The home fans had only just returned to Valley Parade after the appalling tragedy of the fire in '85 that killed 56 supporters. Leeds fans, reacting with their customary sportsmanship to Bradford's second goal, overturned a large takeaway van at the back of the stand and set fire to it. Hundreds of terrified supporters dashed onto the pitch, all the nightmares of the past returning to the forefront of their minds. The FA chairman Bert Millichip later announced that Leeds would not be punished. And then the football establishment wonders why UEFA proceeded so cautiously with our return! The phrases 'senile' and 'old bastards' spring to mind. These Leeds fans, in helpfully illuminating their scumminess to the rest of the world, had succeeded in becoming as unpopular in Britain as Don Revie's team ever was. Well done Leeds. We're sure your ewes were proud of you.

Elsewhere in 1986/87

◻ The Liverpool of British politics, Mrs Thatcher, wins the third in a hat-trick of election victories. The Tories have apparently now been given the country to keep as a result.

◻ Five alleged Chelsea Headhunters get long jail terms of up to 10 years following Operation Own Goal; an apt name since the convictions all run into trouble on appeal. Pity.

◻ 26 Heysel Kopites succeed in blocking their extradition to Belgium in the High Court based on two technical irregularities, this following a fierce campaign on their behalf in 'Pool. In the light of this, does anyone else find Merseyside's demands for the stringing-up of those 'responsible' for Hillsborough rather distasteful? No one is to do time for the Juve manslaughters.

◻ Brian McClair is Scotland's top scorer with 35 goals and is duly voted Player of the Year. Later it emerges that Fergie had been tracking him and plotting his transfer all season. He joins United in the summer for a bargain £850,000.

◻ Lawrie McMenemy, having built an entire career on his one FA Cup win over United, fails yet again at Sunderland. Naturally, this lifetime of under-achievement later makes him perfect for the England No. 2 job. Why didn't we give Geordie-land to the Scots when we had the chance 500 years ago?

◻ Glasgow Rangers continue to disgrace themselves. New player-manager Graeme Sourness – who said on arrival he was joining the biggest club in Britain *after* Man United – gets sent off after 37 minutes of his debut and provokes a mass punch-up. Later, Rangers go out of the UEFA Cup after having two players sent-off in a game screened live all over Europe.

◻ Incidentally, if you're wondering how the sheep molesters were doing, they once again failed to get promoted from Division Two thus making FIVE years of fannying about down there. 'Crowds' at three early season matches got down to 12,000. Such a big club. Such loyal fans.

◻ Just in case you missed it before, CITY WENT DOWN! (again).

◻ Tear-drenched veggieburgers ahoy as The Smiths, Strettie-born, fall apart over the summer; City fan Johnny Marr leaves O.T. veteran Morrissey in the lurch. Indie-music is dead.

◻ A young Frenchman called Eric Cantona signs professional terms with Guy Roux's Auxerre.

1987/88

Football nicknames rarely demonstrate any sort of lyrical wit, usually amounting to the addition of the suffix '-y' to the bloke's name, so Brian McClair being christened 'Choccy' merits some sort of literary award. Actually, it would have been more apt to call him 'Snotty', such was his penchant for shooting greenies out of his nasal torpedo tubes every time a camera turned to him. Even now that he's getting old and slow, he still fires a mean snotball, often with both barrels. On one occasion, you could have sworn that he also managed to fire something out of his ear *simultaneously* – truly a unique talent befitting a man with a college education. One wondered whether this behaviour was some form of footballer's Tourette's syndrome, the disease that causes sufferers to swear, fart and yell involuntarily at the most inopportune moments.

Later it became clear that this was in fact a cunning trick to prevent TV directors zooming in on him after another glaring miss, their desire to show the close-up humiliation of the off-target striker outweighed by the fear of the screen turning mucus-green. Clever bloke, that McClair. As far as we were concerned at the start of the new season, Choccy was already a proven marksman, a Celtic thoroughbred and a bit of a Summer Sale Special bargain at less than a million – from the beginning there was nothing but high hopes and goodwill for him from us. The press had recently unearthed yet another historical albatross to sling around our necks – the rapidly clichéd 'no 20-goal striker since Best'. McClair was to be the terminator of that particular taunt.

On the same day, United were the lucky recipients of the talents of angry Viv Anderson, a cheap stocking-filler from the Highbury bargain basement at £250,000. Many were soon to come to the judgement that Arsenal should've paid *us* to take him on. By all accounts he was a splendid chap to have around and a genuine United-lover to this day but, all too often, watching him play made you wonder if he'd got all his England caps as the result of some botched Equal Opportunities programme. Ironically, given Fergie's stated policy of avoiding ageing or injury-prone players, the 31-year-old Viv was to miss great chunks of the next three seasons after getting crocked. Not for the first time, Alex's actions hadn't quite matched his words.

We didn't know it but the pattern of the next few years was encapsulated in those first summer moves that also saw Glen Hysen snub Alex for the first time; each transfer season, we would habitually pick up a gem, get landed with a tub of lard and get embarrassingly knocked back by some unprincipled greedy bastard of a prima donna. Still, at this point most of us were slightly disappointed that the 'Fergie Purge' the press had convinced us was coming hadn't really amounted to very much, at least in terms of purchases.

Off-loading had proceeded at a pace, of course. Poor Johnny Sivabaek was flogged to St. Etienne, having won the Nikolai Jovanovic Award for his sterling impression of 'nice foreigner hopelessly out of depth in England'. Frank Stapleton, who had seized up alarmingly and was playing as morosely as he behaved off the pitch, went to Ajax, to the relief of the more jocular characters in the dressing room – 'perhaps we can all have a bit of a laugh now' said one. By examining Davenport's strike-rate perhaps? Peter Barnes, to the regret of no one in particular, went back 'home' to City, his appearances in Red being so few as to make it possible to forget the Bluenose was ever here. Terry Gibson, the most laughably wasteful of Ron's

21

sprees, went appropriately to Wimbledon; a net loss of almost half a million for a goal against the Gooners did not represent the best business ever done at Old Trafford. . .

Sadder losses were Gary Bailey and, later, Remi Moses to injury; more controversial were the frees granted at the end of the season to Arthur Albiston, the best full back the modern United has ever had, and Kevin Moran, who has since delighted in proving to Alex that over-30 does not always mean over-the-hill. Hindsight is a wonderful thing; now we realise that if they hadn't been marked for sale, then, Steve Bruce and possibly Pally would not have arrived. But the fact remained that when you added the minor sales in, Fergie sold virtually an entire team in those nine months and hadn't brought in many replacements.

Now even Fergie will admit he went too far, since in pruning so drastically he left the squad dangerously exposed. However, who knows what financial constraints he had been placed under by the Board and how many of these losses were forced upon him to bring in fees and cut wages? Certainly, in December of '87, Fergie was rumbling discontentedly about the lack of money being made available, saying he was 'disappointed in being second best to Liverpool in this respect' and citing his record in dealing at Aberdeen as proof that he 'had respect for money'. This supposed failure to provide Alex with the necessary dosh to compete was to cost us in later seasons.

So United were to kick off the new term with a leaner squad, still containing two names on Fergie's OAP hit-list – Strachan and Davenport. Intriguingly, he'd wanted to sign John Barnes but says he was let down by an inconclusive scouting report. Given what the Gloved One was about to do at Anfield that season, one can only despair at the loss – then, anyway.

Peter Beardsley remains, of course, a continuing source of bitter regret. Not only had Ron allowed the supremely talented toothless hunchback to slip from our grasp a couple of years earlier, now in '87 Liverpool had snapped him up for less than £2 million – after Newcastle had told us they wanted three for him. Months later, the brown-ale-breathed Geordie gets proved to be almost as cantankerous with us over the proposed Gazza deal. They join Notts Forest and Norwich as the clubs most likely to jerk us around in the market. Bastards!

There's little point in hypothesising over what might have been but let's do it nevertheless. Beardsley and Barnes could, quite easily, have joined United that summer. Instead, they went to Anfield to form the basis of the only truly great and entertaining Liverpool side of the '80s. It's blindingly obvious that with them, we'd have walked the title. The irony is that '87/'88, statistically, was our best season of the modern era until then. Runners-up with only five defeats – then a record – and possibly champs in most other seasons and yet...the truth was, as Fergie told Edwards at the time and as most of us accepted, we were not good enough to usurp Liverpool.

Perhaps even more importantly, even if we had won the league, it would not have been in the style that we wished to do it. It seems churlish to say so, given the season's record and the fact we only dropped three points of the last 30, but the terrace mutterings spoke of 'Aberdeen' or, even worse, 'Wimbledon' style football that didn't compare favourably to the cream of the Atkinson era. When Fergie began a more rigorous clearout at the end of the campaign, those marked 'for sale' were bemusedly asking why a runners-up team should be broken up. But to give Alex credit, he had recognised what most of us knew – that this particular collection of players would never get such good results again; the only way was down. Robson conceded the point too; however much he had enjoyed playing with this team, he knew that it would never improve sufficiently to catch Liverpool. These were still, essentially, the remnants of the Atkinson side, most with their best years behind them or so it seemed. A new team for a new era was required.

* * * * *

Still, even if these were performances for old time's sake, at least it was better than 12 months ago. Before Christmas, we only lost twice in the league; McClair had removed any doubts that he might turn out to be Birtles or Brazil and Robbo was the injury-free powerhouse of our dreams. Nevertheless, you struggle to recall any brilliance although the 4-2 win at Hillsborough which never used to be a fruitful hunting ground deserves remembrance, especially given that Walsh and Moran played on in a concussed daze.

Equally indelible was the trip to Upton Park at the end of October which entailed one of the more hair-raising expeditions to a ground that season – how many do you know who made it there and back unscathed? A typical West Ham welcome then, followed by a typical United disaster; Paul McGrath injured and out for months. Less typically, on the pitch Colin Gibson scored the first goal of his season with a deflected free kick right under the massed beer bellies of the Hammers' boot boys. Luvverly.

McGrath's misfortune was ours, of course; Fergie called his loss the turning point of the season. We didn't realise that it was also to be the first step towards the departure of the man who most would agree was the greatest defender of the decade. The only consolation was that Alex was forced into the market, picking up Norwich's Steve Bruce for £825,000 after a protracted wrangle with their sad chairman. Not that he was the first choice – Terry Butcher would've arrived had he not broken his leg. Thank you Lord for that timely intervention. A bid went in for Pally too and it appears we could've had him for far less than we eventually paid out, although in retrospect it's perhaps just as well that he got another 18 months to develop away from the harsh glare of the OT spotlight.

Three weeks after the West Ham bruiser, Loonypool and their collection of dustbin-scavengers arrived at OT, top of the

24

League, on song and looking to settle the debts of '86/'87. They took the lead and for 10 seconds or so there was fear but it soon became apparent that United would NOT lose. Those final minutes before the equaliser were filled with such concerted, cacophonous passion that you just knew the goal was coming.

The United Road paddock, though past its mid-'80s peak, was playing a blinder whilst K-Stand was beginning to stir for the first time. As Jesper's corner swung over, Scouse defenders were clearly off their heads on a panic-high; Norm – who else? – swivelled to score through The Clown's legs, leaving Craig Johnston on the line as Prat of the Day. And all right under the pustular noses of the Scouse horde in the paddock, who reacted in time-honoured fashion by pelting missiles at Norm and the boys. None reached its target incidentally; presumably too many arm muscles shrivelled by smack injections in there.

In fact, we should've won that game. Choccy's double ensured that we beat the other Scouse visitors at Christmas but we remained too many points behind to consider the title a serious prospect. Once again, all hopes resided in the cups.

By February 20th, such hopes had been extinguished. Firstly the worst week of the season in mid-January had seen us succumb at home the Saints; four days later, a dreadful first half that resembled the previous season's night at the Dell saw us go out of the League Cup to Oxford – the sort of club to whom United should never lose whatever the circumstances.

The FA Cup exit was far worse, mainly because it seemed so cruelly unjust. We'd won at Highbury only five matches before when Strachan had jinked, shimmied and struck with one of the goals of the season; we'd won five of the last six away breathing new life into 'Jingle Bells' and even Liam O'Brien was finding the target. We then proceeded to play in the first half as if all the players were strangers meeting at a party, fumbling introductions and passes as Arsenal scored twice. Presumably someone tipped a bag of speed into the brew at the break because we tore them apart; after Choccy's volley and a couple of goal-line clearances, Norm won us a spot-kick to level it with three minutes to go. Or so we thought. McClair blasted it over the bar and we were out. End of season. End, temporarily, of love affair with Choccy. *Not* the end, unfortunately, of our troubles with penalties.

Choccy at Highbury '88

* * * * *

Meanwhile, behind the scenes, the in-club entertainment was being provided by the Norm and Paul Roadshow. A spectacularly indulgent tour by the duo of Manchester's nighteries in the week before the game at Loftus Road could hardly fail to capture the attention of the locals – or Alex Ferguson, who was receiving daily updates on the 'phone from City fans. Apparently it was at this point that Alex resolved to sell McGrath. Considering the circumstances, the team did well to win 2-0.

Two months later, the Black Pearl of Inchinore almost

26

became the Bloodied Corpse of Old Trafford when Paul's post-bender driving jaunt ended wrapped around a tree and thence to hospital. The magistrates' intervention meant that Paul was off the road as well as off the pitch but, at least, the pubs were still available. Although Norm and Paul's discontent was not to become public until April, in fact they both had made secret requests to leave as early as October; it was far too simplistic to suggest, as was done later, that Fergie had simply wanted to get rid of them from the off. But when the official request did come, the reporting of it was such that some on the terraces took a dim view. During the warm-up and game when Luton came for their customary thrashing in April, you could quite clearly hear chants of 'you only want the money' directed at Norm on the bench as well as booing of McGrath. It was a grim moment.

In the midst of that statistically excellent end-of-season run which narrowed the deficit at the top to a flattering eight points, there was a golden 10 days around Easter. The East End ejaculates were dispatched 3-1 featuring a brilliant solo Strachan goal, McClair got a hat-trick in the demolition of Derby and then it was on to Anfield. It was to be the only game of the last eight that we failed to win but it many ways it remains the outstandingly delectable memory of the season.

If you take the outpourings from the likes of the Echo and Mersey's local radio whinge-a-thon 'phone-ins as an indicator of Liverpudlian mentality, by April '88 their manic loathing of all things Mancunian had reached a zenith. Of course, it must have been most aggravating for the Mickeys that every time a clash of the Reds came around, the national media invariably harked upon the Scouses' inability to do United. Come the Easter clash, the banks of rat-scoffers on the Kop were convinced that at last, United were to be put in their place.

The euphoria of Robbo's nicely-slotted opener right in front of us was short-lived. By the middle of the second half we were in a full-on Doomsday Scenario. Down 3-1, down to 10 men and apparently down and out. Steve McMahon had spent the entire game roaming around hacking limbs to pieces, utterly unmolested by the ref who nevertheless found Colin Gibson's minor transgressions enough to warrant an early bath. This was turning into the archetypal Anfield Experience – a total travesty of justice with organised gamesmanship benevolently supervised by a supine official. Then off the bench came Norm.

With just two challenges, the Terminator removed Barnes and McMahon from the equation altogether. McMahon in particular was honoured to receive one of Norm's very special tackles, reserved for those who've been living by the sword and who now must also die by the sword. It was a beautifully executed piece of vigilante justice; from that moment on, the entire 'Pool team retreated like frightened punks in a Dirty Harry movie. Jimmy Hill and the rest of the BBC branch of the L.S.C. entered the stratosphere of apoplectic outrage, their sanctimony all the more disgusting given their tacit approval of McMahon's behaviour. Robbo pulled one back and then Strachan, in a timeless moment, strode through to bury number three in the back of the Kop net. Jigging insouciantly over to the stunned granny-stabbers, he delightfully mimicked the smoking of a celebratory cigar in a two-fingered gesture that carried its own subtext. 3-3 and we could've won it but for McClair's miss.

Yet another season had passed in which Liverpool proclaimed themselves the best but failed to prove it against their most despised rivals. How very upsetting for them. It was immensely gratifying to see the ill-feeling between the supporters spill out to infect the managers afterwards – such a pleasant change from the nauseating 'let's be pals' act we'd often got from the Clubs' establishments. Fergie delighted every manager who'd ever been to Anfield in the '80s by telling it how it was; that the atmosphere of intimidation, the bully boy tactics of the Liverpool team and the abysmal, crowd-pleasing refereeing at that ground made a fair contest impossible. As Alex so pithily put it, 'teams leave here choking back the vomit'.

At this point in the Anfield tunnel, up skulked Dalglish himself, offspring in arms, to opine that more sense would be gained from addressing the toddler. How charming of him to involve his innocent daughter in a nasty adult argument. Fergie's reply went unbroadcast but the 'off' was audible at least. It was the first time that the nation at large became aware of the personal antipathy between the two men which had apparently solidified when Fergie, as Scotland manager for the '86 World Cup, had left out Hansen thus prompting very close personal chum Kenny into a vendetta against Fergie. Such emotionalism! – you'd think they were married or something.

Since the Anfield bust-up, Fergie appears to have risen above this sort of thing, but not Dalglish so it seems. At a press conference before last season's clash, so *The Guardian* reported, the big bummed Blackburn boss astonished assembled hacks by ranting at length about United, leaving all present in no doubt that the feud was very much alive. This makes Kenny's coy, cooing comments congratulating 'Grandfather Fergie' after our title retention all the more nauseating – a prime piece of SMAC. As Fergie would say, 'choke back the vomit!'

* * * * *

It was about this time when the strangest of phenomena made their appearance on our terraces – inflatable skeletons. Has there been a convincing explanation as to why these oddities in particular started showing up at games? Red-haters were quick to spread the legend that these were, in fact, a sick reference to the departed Bill Shankly which would have been more credible had not Shanks been dead for seven years. The inflatable craze was eventually picked up by the media who trumpetted this as a manifestation of a new terrace culture based on surrealist pre-Reeves good humour and more likely fuelled by the new aroma that was crowding out the Bovril fumes – cannabis smoke.

City fans were keen to claim credit for this development as

proof that they were the street-cred style originators of the footie world though it's more likely they stole it from some lower division wasters just as they did with 'Blue Moon'. Nevertheless, as home of many of the city's drug-dealing fraternity, Maine Rd might have a claim. But who cares? It's a sad situation when your pretensions to greatness are based on plastic bananas instead of silver trophies.

Potheads at football, however, were far more interesting. Scruffy and baggy had already been in around Manchester for a few seasons, the first summer of love was on its way and Madchester was a year from exploding into international consciousness. Wildly flapping flares were being retrieved from attics; truly floppy fringes to match voluminous T-shirts were becoming an increasingly common sight around town. Manchester had always been *the* centre of excellence for music and a prime breeding ground for the cross-fertilisation of music and footie – it was only natural that the habits of the club should be imported into the stadium.

Lugging four-packs was *passé*; packing a 'teenth and some skins was the thing. It would be a gross exaggeration to claim half of Old Trafford would spend much of the next couple of seasons off its collective face but there were times, looking at the sand-dunes by the goals, that you felt there was more grass in the stands than on the pitch. It's been said elsewhere that it would be too pat to draw a direct causal link between the decline of aggro and the rise of the zine-reading, baggy-bedecked, mellowed-out fan but it certainly helped change the general atmosphere. Nevertheless, the danger in imagining that late '80s Manchester was one huge love-in was perfectly illustrated by the punch-up at Maine Road in '89 – hardly the expected behaviour of blissed-out tokers was it?

Still, how welcome is Manchester's ability to produce musical palliatives when the football's making you suffer. When Dave Sexton was depressing you to the depths, you could go home, listen to Joy Division and wallow in self-pity for a bit before cheering up when you realised that however bad United were playing, at least you weren't as screwed up as Ian Curtis. When Hughes was on his way to Barca and United were plummeting, you could slap 'The Queen Is Dead' on, rediscover your black sense of humour and laugh bitterly about the cruelty of life. And now, bored and appalled by the torpor that United so often induced between '88 and '90, you could at least find pure escape at nights, courtesy of the local man and the trip-out of 'Resurrection'.

Conversely, when the game is good, the music is dead; check out the lack of Manc rock gods in the '60s or the bleakness of today. Who's got time to spend months in subterranean recording studios when there's top footie to follow? (Obviously, this theory falls apart if you reckon Bluenoses Oasis are any good – though if you do, you've clearly taken *too many* drugs)

Incidentally, whilst on the drugs subject, it's a fair bet that Moss Side ran out of anti-depressants after City's 4-0 Cup KO at the hands of Liverpool, especially after the pre-quarter final 'we're going to Wembley and you're not' hype from the Blues.

31

Happily, this was not to be the last time that City let four in at home in a last-eight Cup tie after excessive Bluenose hype. Mouthy Maine Roaders have never really learned that talking hard before a match serves only as a hostage to fortune, as Pitbull Phelan was the latest to discover last April.

Getting as far away as possible from drugs altogether, a 16-year-old Lee Sharpe was signed from Torquay during the season for a £125,000 deposit – surely the bargain of the decade. However, at the time, the excited talk was of a possible return from exile for Mark Hughes who had been continually monitored throughout his sojourn in Munich. Also under Alex's consideration was Paul Gascoigne, about whom nego-tiations had begun as early as October. In the end, not even Bobby Charlton could convince Edwards to take on Gazza. He had demanded the most extravagant personal terms in the history of British football but Tottenham had met them whereas United did not.

Edwards was running a fairly hefty debt at this point – £2.5 million by the start of '88/'89 – and was probably reluctant to add to it especially since his own income was dependent on the club's finances. The failure to buy Gazza, however, was surely a classic case of short-termism. Liverpool had gone heavily into debt for their purchases in '87 but had easily recouped the outlay from the profits success brought. The old adage of capitalism – you've got to speculate to accumulate – seems to have been forgotten by the Board. To think that we could have had those two glorious seasons of Gazza and then trousered five or six million Lazio pounds...

Unfortunately, instead of signing Gazza, the 'highlight' of United's financial season was the sale of a basketball club in March which had lost United at least £0.25 million. Earlier, the club newspaper *ManU News*, an ill-conceived venture that was even more tedious a read than the programme, folded after three issues, as predicted by all who read the first edition. However, the new membership scheme started in '87 was proving to be a 'success' if not a particularly popular venture.

The Club had launched it on a wave of bullshit about the fabulous European giants' schemes which raised squillions in advance cash and added to the cohesion of the club and supporters. What wasn't emphasised is that in many clubs on the continent, membership has a real meaning and purpose – fans get to elect officials, take policy decisions and become an unignorable force of opinion. Naturally, there was no chance of us receiving that sort of respect from United; the scheme has basically become a useful method of social control that helps minimise dissidence – and a source of an up-front million each season. Thank you so much.

* * * * *

The jocular highlight of an otherwise dour season was the arrest of Clayton 'Sunbed' Blackmore for alleged sexual impropriety on a trip to North America. The affair quickly blew over without coming to a climax (gwoop, gwoop) but overnight the Clayton Cult had firmly established itself. Blackmore was in the middle of his "best" season yet, having had a dozen games in each of the previous years filling in whatever holes were required in the team (fnar, fnar). Like most Welsh players of his type, he was a slightly dodgy defender with midfield pretensions. What is it about Welsh backs? Wales always manage to produce glamorous, exciting forward lines yet their back four is invariably stuffed with Second Division nonentities notable only for their sudden absence when foreign strikers are bearing down in packs on Neville Southall. Undoubtedly, this is due to the genetics of rugby; somewhere in their chromosomes, ancestral forces push Welsh defenders up-field in search of far corner tries. This might also explain their propensity to handle the ball at crucial moments, or so Joe Jordan claimed in 1977 anyway.

In the absence of any serious competition, Clayton became the Sex God of Old Trafford, famed for his physique, all-year tan and chat-up lines. How the girls adored his long, lean thighs, his chiselled lantern jaw, those perfectly rounded cheekbones, the finely sculptured upper torso...Nurse! Nurse! Bring the vat of bromide and some Kleenex! As a player, however, he always bore the air of a sexy temporary secretary continually on the verge of being replaced by a dowdier but more effective performer; only in '90/'91 did he truly seem at ease. The girls may have sighed for Sunbed but only his occasional blistering free kicks brought sexual excitement to the lads. Clayton has settled down now at last, but sadly his home is the desolate wasteland of the Endsleigh League.

Still, as with that other perennial non-performer, Les Sealey, Clayton's cult appeal remains undimmed – the legend of the Sunbed King is secure. Sunbed fans can see their hero at Ayresome Park and in the final series of 'Minder' under the stage name Gary Webster.

As the season ended with a fondly-remembered Cup Final, we looked forward to the Euro Championships in Germany and dreamed of Hughes and McClair together in the autumn. Things can only get better. Wrong again.

Elsewhere in 1987/88

◻ David Pleat brings a new meaning to 'scouting for talent' and gets sacked by Spurs who are, of course, known for their law-abiding nature...

◻ Sourness and his moustache get sent off for the third time in a year and receive a five-match ban. Clearly his sense of sportsmanship is already marking him out as a future Scouse boss. Rangers 'stars' Woods and Butcher get done in court for their part in an old firm punch-up. *Plus ça change.*

◻ Arsenal find out what it's like to lose at Wembley in the last minute; ex-Red Ashley Grimes aids the revenge for '79.

◻ Two unique events in the FA Cup Final; Liverpool suffer a cruel refereeing decision and 'Dave Beasant' appears in the same sentence as the word 'hero'.

◻ Chelsea lose to Boro in the relegation play-offs. Typically, they invade the pitch, beat up Boro fans, attack ambulance-men with stones and bottles and have 102 of their number arrested.

◻ Ian Rush spends the year at Juventus. In Turin the word *Rush* enters the lingo – it means 'crap'. Gonzo returns to describe his ordeal thus: "It was like being in a foreign country, like."

◻ Several Scousers at Wembley on touted tickets later discover they came from Bobby Charlton's allocation. Oops.

◻ England embarrass the nation in Germany; Robbo is the only decent performer. No change there then. At least the Krauts don't win it though.

◻ Merseysiders greet Liverpool new-boy John Barnes with a hail of bananas. Ooh, that Scouse shining wit.

◻ New star of French football Eric Cantona scores on his debut for the national team.

K STAND

ACCORDING TO OTHER CLUBS FANZINES, THE MOST FEARED SEATED STAND IN ENGLAND. TOTALLY LOYAL, REASONABLE AND MUCH MALIGNED FANS WHOSE ONLY THOUGHTS ARE FOR THE COMFORT OF THE VISITORS BELOW. FAV. GAMES LIVERPOOL, EVERTON, AND FIRST TIME VISITORS WHO MISTAKE AT THEIR PERIL, K FOR THE AWAY SEATED SECTION.

J — FOR UNITED FANS WHO LIKE TO HIDE IN CORNERS

SCOREBOARD END

AWAY FANS ONLY THESE DAYS IF THEY BOTHER TURNING UP OCCUPIED IN THE 70's BY THE COCKNEY REDS WHO ENJOYED MAKING LIFE UNBEARABLE FOR THOSE WHO CAME. FAV GAME-SUNDERLAND DIV II WHEN THEIR FANS RAN

A DIRECT RESULT OF THE SEXTON YEARS WHEN BORED REDS EVERYWHERE TURNED AWAY FROM O.T. TO THEIR WIVES/GIRLFRIENDS. FAVOURITE GAME-FOREST DEC. 17TH 1977. ONE OF THE EDITORS HAS TWO KIDS THANKS TO THIS ONE

© RED ISSUE 88

OLD TRAFFORD · 88

SCOREBOARD PADDOCK

OLD DOCKERS CONGREGATE HERE TO REMINISCE ON DAYS SPENT WEARING DONKEY JACKETS. FAV. GAME-CHELSEA SEPT 17TH 1977

G + H — COLLECTIVELY THIS LOT COULD DO WITH NEW WATCHES. THEY SEEM TO THINK THE GAME FINISHES AT 4-15 FULL OF OLD CODGERS WHO CLAIM THEY'VE SEEN IT ALL. BUT ARE RARELY SEEN OUTSIDE MANCHESTER. FAVOURITE GAME BARCELONA — THEY ACTUALLY STOOD WHEN WE SCORED

UNITED ROAD

DOUBTFUL IF THERE'S AN IQ OF 100 BETWEEN THE LOT OF THEM. HOWEVER TO BE CONGRATULATED FOR BEING THE START OF GIBSON'S ABUSE

A B C D — THIS LOT HAVE SEEN IT ALL. WE WERE GOING TO ABUSE THEM BUT ONE OF THE EDITORS FATHERS SITS HERE SO WE THOUGHT IT BEST LEFT ALONE

CABBAGE PATCH

F — IF YOU'RE SAT HERE, CHANCES ARE IT WAS A FREE TICKET. WORST VIEW AND WEATHER CONDITIONS TO MATCH

DEVELOPMENT PLANS INCLUDE THE REMOVAL OF THE 'KEEP QUIET' SIGNS.

STRETFORD END

KNOWN AS THE LIBRARY? WE HOPE KNIGHTONS

STRETFORD PADDOCK

LAST FEW REMNANTS OF DOC'S RED ARMY. BIGGEST THRILL THESE DAYS IS WATCHING THE UNITED HISTORY VIDEO.

E — ER, WELL WHAT CAN YOU SAY REALLY. DEFINITE FIRE HAZARD — TIME IT WAS PULLED DOWN.

1988/89

The cult of the Red Devil, like all other religions, is hugely dependent on a nebulous concept you might dimly recall from ancient RE lessons – the leap of faith. Basically, it's the ability to believe in the incredible without really having any concrete evidence that your faith is well founded. During many a summer in the last 20 years, starry-eyed, frenziedly-optimistic Reds have happily thrown themselves forward in just such a leap of faith, convincing themselves that *this* year would see the Holy Grail achieved. Months later would come the miserable reflections on failure, the cold-light realisation that we'd fooled ourselves once more.

So it was to be in '88/'89. The untrammelled joy we felt upon the return of the Prodigal Son from Barca via Munich had suffused our souls to such an extent that we were immune to the doom-laden realities of our situation. Knicker-wettingly thrilled by the prospect of an improved Hughes linking up with hotshot McClair, we ignored the harsh facts that our squad was undermanned, three of our best players were hankering for new pastures and Big Kev had been mistakenly released. Furthermore, as we were soon to realise, our defence had been infected by a cancer; Dennis Potter called his tumour Rupert Murdoch – ours was called Jim Leighton. It was to eat away at our body for the next two seasons.

When you consider it in retrospect, what on earth were we doing signing a Scottish goalkeeper? They had been a music-hall joke for 20 years, their awfulness such a well-established cliché that only saddoes like Greavsie still bothered to mention it. No English clubs ever signed these misbegotten creatures for the simple reason that they ARE all abysmal; it's virtually genetic. One day they'll discover that there's a goalkeeping chromosome and that it's always hideously deformed north of the border. Alex has often been quoted as claiming, only half-jokingly, that the Scots are the master race – an interesting theory given the Scots' World Cup performances against such Aryan supermen as Costa Rica – and not for the first time, United were to suffer the consequences of the manager's unhinged Scotophilia.

Consequently, Chris Turner was shown the door and Graeme Hogg went with him; by November Olsen was in France, Davenport in Middlesboro and Liam O'Brien on Tyneside. With Arthur and Kev gone already, that made seven departures with only four replacements: Hughes, Leighton, Donaghy and Milne. Frankly, our old friends Mal and Ralph scarcely count as 'replacements'; they'd be hard pushed to keep Tommy Jackson out of a side. Jim, of course, counts as a positive liability. In real terms, we'd sold seven and gained one. As we were soon to discover, it would only take a couple of injuries in such a squad to throw the season into utter disarray.

Donaghy was no cheapo stand-in; he'd set us back £750,000 when we needed a replacement for the injured McGrath. Already 28 and arguably past his peak, he'd have been unnecessary had we kept Kev for another season. And this after Fergie had made it clear he was out to *sell* all the merely average, ageing players. Mal was not, needless to say, destined to become an OT God.

Ralph Milne. A name from your nightmares. Be very, very afraid. The Doc said of him that milk could turn faster – and that was one of the nicest comments aimed at the Bristolian 'winger'. Ralph graduated straight into the elite Boo Boys Target Club which expanded rapidly throughout the season. Fergie notes huffily in his book that 'stop-gap signings' never get a chance at OT – too bloody right! That a club of United's size and ample resources should ever be forced into trawling lower divisions for cheap crud to provide cover in a threadbare squad is totally unacceptable. The signing was an unmitigated disaster, naturally.

It is, of course, a common occurrence to hear insiders slating the OT faithful for 'getting at' certain players. We are told off like schoolboys who've farted in assembly for daring to express our disapproval at any manager's decisions. We are told that we never gave so-and-so a chance, or that we 'destroyed' someone's career; we ought to shut our mouths and let the omniscient boss do as he sees fit. This is exactly the sort of expression of attitude that makes you want to machine-gun the press box. Since we pay the wages of everyone at the Club, we above all others have the right to do our best to get a player dumped if we decide that is what's necessary.

Managers are neither infallible nor unbiased – most bosses will be loathe to admit they've bought a dud and will generally play him till the bitterest of ends to prove they were right. In such circumstances, the fans are the ones putting the Club's interest first. Besides, it is a calumny to suggest that we never give lads a chance. By and large, we somehow instinctively know whether a player is right for United or not. Robbo, Incey, Pally and Keane all had uncertain starts at OT but we were the embodiment of patience, secure in *our* knowledge that they would turn out fine.

But there are times when we conclude that someone is not and never will be up to the standard required when it becomes almost our duty to get him off the pitch. Why did we take such an instant dislike to Milne and others? Because it saved time. The game's wiseacres rarely acknowledge that we have a top record in sussing out the duffers; note that in almost every case where the body of fans has rejected some transplanted player, management has eventually conceded the point and sold him. We couldn't care less what the journos, ex-players and commentators think of us; we know we're the best judges and, frankly, as the wage-payers, our opinion is the most important of all. The fact is that Alex bought badly that season and we were only to happy to let him know it.

* * * * *

Usually, it was not until mid-winter that United's campaigns got wrecked by injuries but this time Fate got its retaliation in first by awarding us a nice crock of injuries before the season even kicked off. Norm was to miss all but six games, an unjustly inglorious anti-climax to such a fabulous career. Less regrettable was the lengthy absence of Viv thus reducing swearing at OT by 50% and allowing Lee Sharpe into the team. Duxbury and McGrath both missed over half the season; with the squad stripped down to basics, how could we hope to challenge for anything?

We waited for further purchases but none came; Cruyff offered us Lineker for £2.5 million in November but we apparently couldn't afford it. Re-read that sentence. Remind yourself we'd only scored 13 in 11 matches and still had an average gate of 44,000. What does that tell you about the MUFC Board in 1988? Despair was back in fashion with a vengeance. The sad truth was that up-front, things were not working out as expected; by the end of November, McClair had only scored twice in the League although Hughesy after a shaky start was already on eight. Throughout the season, they never managed to hit good form simultaneously – one always seemed to be 'carrying' the other.

The Great Hughes Myth – that he was allegedly impossible to play off – began to be circulated by our enemies. Nevertheless, both players ended up with 16 goals and Hughes was voted Player of the Year which is hardly a terrible return from a first season together. The real problem was that Robbo apart, we were getting nothing in the net from midfield and that the team as a whole was decimated by casualties. Looking at the season review in the last programme was instructive; what a mess the team line-ups were in a year when getting an unchanged 11 from match-to-match was a triumph in itself.

After a stuttering start, however, including defeat to a Barnes penalty in a downtrodden, idiotically-scheduled game at Anfield, the prospects looked brightish for a while. A hat-trick of wins culminated in a hugely satisfying win against the Hammers that saw Hughes score his first goal since his return and the rare sight of a brilliant Davenport effort; Hughes then scored a scintillating swivelling net-buster at Spurs but we only took a point – from there it was downhill all the way. We won only one more game before Christmas. Eight League draws and a defeat was hardly the form of aspirant champions.

Hughesy's athletic cheeky goal over Southall's despairing clutch at our Gwladys Street end and his bottom-corner cracker at the Baseball ground are the only moments of devilish flamboyance from those grim months. Strachan seemed past it, Olsen was gone and a settled defence was a distant memory. Alarmingly, Leighton was beginning to give us palpitations after a statistically good start – five clean sheets in six. Against the Saints he committed a blunder as hideous as he was, somehow conspiring to thrust a harmless high ball into our net with no one in the vicinity. It was the TV comedy highlight of the week, fondly remembered by all connoisseurs of Scottish guardianship.

By this time, United were already out of one Cup. Hacked off the pitch by a Wimbledon at their most Neanderthal, a match handled with all the minimal competence at Brian Hill's command, chief Womble Fashanu enacted a premature audition for 'Gladiators' by slamming Viv in the tunnel; general marauding ensued whilst the ref cowered in his dressing room. Viv not only got three stitches but the FA saw fit to throw in a fine and a ban on top, swayed pathetically by Fashanu's impression of Bambi at the disciplinary hearing. Once again, the FA displayed their ability to bring the game into disrepute all by themselves. Tossers!

Christmas arrived as we came home from defeats at Highfield Road and Highbury; Santa's sack, it seemed, had nothing in it for United but socks. The Bank Holidays would see Forest and Liverpool at OT, both at the top of their game. United were stumbling, injury-laden and apparently out of luck; many of us walked down the Warwick Road with dread in our hearts.

42

The atmosphere was redolent of the late '70s Yuletides when these two teams had come to OT and won three or four-nil, thus wrecking our festive seasons completely; many a newly-unwrapped puppy got a kicking in those dark days. We didn't yet know that this Christmas would be illuminated by the new-born young saviours later christened the Fergie Fledglings.

Russell Beardsmore, Lee Sharpe, Lee Martin, Tony Gill and later Deniol Graham, Mark Robins and Jules Maiorana were all drafted in at various stages of the next few weeks to rescue United from an injury crisis largely of the club's own making. Scarcely out of school uniform, usually totally inexperienced and thrown into a creaking, inconsistent team, they rose magnificently to the challenge in a fashion we had no right to expect. Without getting too sloppily homosexual about it, the OT faithful fell instantly in love with them all. We forgave every mistake, exalted their every success and rejoiced in their untempered youthful vigour and spirit. They gave us our most treasured moments of the season, they saved us from a Christmas stuffing and they put us on the road to Wembley, or so we thought. Above all, their appearance fulfilled the desire that lies within every Red, a longing instilled in the fans since the '50s and that is still there in these mega deal superstar times – that nothing beats the thrill of watching a young unknown, bred by United and filled with the Red Devil ideology, coming into the team and staking his claim. Now suddenly, as the proverbial silver-lining to the injury-crisis cloud, we had half a dozen of these boys swamping the opposition.

As a Boxing Day *hors-d'oeuvre*, Forest were well-beaten 2-0 with even Ralphie Milne entering the spirit of things by, shockingly, scoring the first. The main course on New Year's Day was Roasted Scouse Rat, done to a turn by Russell Beardsmore & Co and beamed live to a delighted nation. Beardsmore, this gawky frail novice with the heart of a lion and the feet of an angel, was a total revelation; Lee Sharpe seemed to be playing in three positions at once, all brilliantly. Even though Strachan had limped off, to be replaced by an impressive Robins, and even though Barnes gave them an unjustified 70th minute lead, the United tide still threatened to engulf the Mickeys at any moment.

In a 10-minute spell of complete ecstasy, Choccy, Hughes and Beardsmore stuffed three goals in the Stretford End net in the midst of a hurricane of attacking force. It was utter devastation; it really could've been five or six by the end. Surely that third goal must be burned into every Red's cerebral cortex for eternity; Sharpe somehow squeezing that cross over from the byline, dropping eventually to the Man of the Match himself, the ball nestling in the corner of a split-second later amidst scenes of orgasmic abandon across the stadium. The joyous roar that greeted the goal was surely never matched again until Brucie's winner against Wednesday over four years later. After the final whistle, as the Scouse went off in a state of shock, Reds simply floated out of the ground; outside the Haç, you'd never seen so many star-filled eyes. Of all our Scousebusting triumphs, few can have matched the emotional intensity of this one.

For the next two months, the passion of the Fledglings carried us forward on a roller-coaster ride that seemed destined to end at the Twin Towers. The older players seemed to have been inspired by the example set by the youngsters; for the first time since Fergie's arrival, we could honestly say we were seeing proper United football at last. In an epic Cup replay at Loftus Road, Tony Gill's thunderous shot took us into extra-time in which Deniol Graham got a second for a 2-2 draw. We played with such élan, running incessantly at opponents and fighting in every corner – the performance lifted the entire club. We won six on the trot after that including three and four goal wins in the Cup that set off a mass outbreak of Wembley fever. For the first time since 1967, we won at West Ham, Strachan playing the game of his season and Choccy scoring a memorable goal at their end. We even won again at Hillsborough, for so long a bogey ground, now McClair's happiest hunting-ground. With the dispatch of Bournemouth, Forest were our sole obstacle to our progressing to the semis. The modern United never loses domestic semi-finals; we were as good as at Wembley itself.

On March 18th, the season's hopes turned to dust. Brian Hill Forest beat United 1-0 at OT and that was that. We had dominated the game and finally got the ball in the net when McClair forced McGrath's header over the line. Forest eyes looked up to the heavens in desolation; the ground erupted, it was 1-1 at last. Brian Hill, standing virtually next to the post, refused to give the goal. Pictures later proved without doubt that not only was the ball over the line, it was at least six inches into the goal. As far as is known, Hill has never admitted his error or offered an apology for his gross mistake; is it any wonder that Fergie later sought to have this official barred from United games? What possible explanation can there be for such a ridiculous piece of officiating? I'm sure Eric Cantona could come up with one for us; libel laws prevent further suggestions here. All we can do is grant him the Courtney Award for Ref Most Likely To Incite A Riot and dream fondly of Kettering Reds paying him a visit en masse one fine day...

The final two months were purgatory. The Cup KO was a knife in the stomach for fans and players alike. Within days, it was revealed that Strachan had been sold to Leeds, which just rounded off a miserable week quite neatly. Strach had not been at his best all year and had almost gone to Lens in August anyway; later he was to complain that Fergie had failed to motivate him or convince him that he had a future at OT, which Alex vehemently rejected, adding caustically that a well-paid star at United shouldn't need 'motivating' anyhow. If we had known then what Strachan was to accomplish at Leeds, our displeasure would have been all the greater; as it was, we were scarcely happy to lose such a talented play-maker who'd been at the centre of the Atkinson firmament.

The season dwindled down to a nihilistic nothingness. We lost eight games in two months; not a single United player found the target in April. Even the Fledglings began to pick up injuries and lose both heart and stamina. The part-timers vanished from the stadium and took a few erstwhile die-hards with them – only 23,000 turned up for the Wimbledon game. The football reverted to pre-Fledgling stodge – tired, limp and passion-free; those of us who'd remained couldn't decide whom we loathed most – the 'fans' who'd deserted us, the players who'd seemingly given up, the Board for selling Strachan and not buying anyone or the manager for his apparent lack of motivatory skill. It was simply bloody awful. Towards the end of the season, the Club pulled a final symbolic stroke by banning inflatables. How apt – how dare we enjoy ourselves?! This was Old Trafford, late '80s style – abandon humour all ye who enter. For once, you looked forward to the cricket season.

*   *   *   *   *

To be frank, there were only three highlights worth recalling from this disappointing season; the glorious exploits of Fergie's Fledglings, Arsenal's winner at Anfield and, from February, the emergence of *Red Issue*.

Although not the first United fanzine – that honour belongs to *Red News* – *Red Issue* has become the definitive United zine and, apparently, a national market-leader. More importantly, it can legitimately claim to be the incarnation of the Old Trafford terrace spirit; for many of the hard-core Reds who are *RI*'s target audience, the mag truly acts as their voice – a pure expression of Red opinion and humour.

'Veg' and 'Zar', the thirty-something K-Standers who still edit *RI* together, had originally been contributors to *Red News* before they split due to the zine equivalent of musical differences; jointly embracing a common 'sick' sense of humour and a belief in their abilities to produce a street-wise, funny and scabrous mag for true Reds, they started flogging the first issue at the Bournemouth Cup game and have continued to publish in an unbroken run ever since, usually running to 10 issues a season. Now, of course, the mag is securely embedded in the terrace culture – a big seller that is professionally produced, available at all sorts of outlets and has spawned its own travel outfit, T-shirt spin-offs and the like, as well as inspiring other United zines. Despite this impressive growth, it has scarcely strayed from its founding principles, remaining firmly anti-establishment, thankfully politically incorrect and full of the passion, bile and gratuitously tasteless humour that we all like to see.

Naturally, this belching, merciless and robustly die-hard beast has often been greeted with horror by moralising tight-arses and rival fans everywhere. A typical response to an early edition was a lump of excrement shoved through Veg's letter-box which thus confirmed to the editors that they must be doing something right. Being on the cutting edge of the zine movement has brought ritual condemnation from other zines, presumably a product of jealousy since *RI* must be the most plagiarised zine in existence. The mainstream media have, for their part, objected to everything that makes *RI* such a top read – its vulgarity, language and savage contempt for our dearest rivals. Of course, what such commentators are really objecting to is the nature of the *reader* rather than the mag itself; the sort of namby-pamby bourgeois prude who slates *RI* in the press is actually expressing his distaste for the working-class terrace Red to whom *RI* is not in the least 'offensive'.

Such critics can thus be safely ignored; in fact, their outrage is to be wholly welcomed. As the editors cheerfully relate, *RI* received its biggest sales boost ever in March 1990 when the *Manc Evening News* filled its back page on the eve of the Scouse game with a piece condemning the mag's 'disgusting' content and reprehensible abuse of our Mickey friends. Next day at the game, droves of punters turned up to fill their pockets with *Red Ish*, prompted by this 'recommendation' – what sweet irony. Similarly, when *The Sunday Times* made *Red Issue* 'Worst Zine of the Year', the editors promptly slapped a banner on the cover for the rest of the season proclaiming the fact – what better evidence of the excellence of *Red Ish* than the fact that Murdoch's pig-sty loathed it?

It's often said that all fanzines have declined, that they're not as funny as they used to be and that the 'serious' side to their mission – to provide an expression of fans views on the game's pressing issues – is no longer as relevant now that these opinions are known. There's also the suggestion that the zines have lost their ideals and are now part of the establishment. As far as *RI* is concerned, the editors accept that it's harder work now to be original; at the beginning, zines had 20 years of unexpressed pent-up gags and opinions to draw on which have long since been exhausted. But whilst *RI* may be inconsistent, dependent as it is on the input flow from contributors, it could not be argued that *RI* at its best is somehow 'inferior' to what went before.

Certainly, *RI* cannot be accused of losing its ideals; it remains as far away from the Club hierarchy as ever and is a constant, conscience-driven thorn in the flesh of the establishment at OT. Not many other zines could claim to be so healthy. Veg reserves particular contempt for City's mags such as *King of the Tampax* (sic): "Pathetic – who wants to read eight pages of interview with some pop group manager who's a part-time fan?" and finds them failing when they come to the acid test – how much do they get under the skin of their rivals? "City's just don't hack it; at least Bolton's really annoys you and makes you think 'you Bolton bastards' – then you realise they've done a good job, and you've got to say well done to them."

Generously, the editors praise Leeds fans' *The Square Ball* for their improvement since the days they were vilified for plagiarism and recognises what a good mag *United We Stand* has become. But in general, they feel satisfied that *RI* has maintained a qualitative edge, reckoning this gut feeling is probably correct because in practice, they never read anything in rival mags that would be worth nicking!

The editors could be excused if they were to feel self-satisfied and smug about their success but both are loathe to make any sort of self-aggrandising claims for themselves or the mag. Particular contempt is reserved for the City zine editor who encourages talk of his possible appointment to the City board as a fans' spokesman – "Who does he think he is? Editors don't *represent* anyone." When asked about what *RI* has achieved, there are no pretentious claims or high-blown sociological theories about the fanzine movement. In fact, the only event the editors would be happy to be credited for is the dropping of Leighton in 1990, citing the moment when Sealey emerged from the Wembley tunnel as one of the highlights of their decade: "I suppose it's sad that it led to the destruction of his career but sod it, Jim Leighton *needed* to be destroyed!"

Of course, the difficulty in evaluating what *Red Ish* has influenced is immense. The Club have taken decisions or sold players after long *RI* campaigns but who is to say how much weight the mag carried with the board or manager? We know it's read inside the Club, but that's all. One must suspect, however, that the zines have effected some change in mentality at OT. It does appear that PR in general and appealing populis-tically to terrace opinion has become more of a priority post-'89. And not before time.

That doesn't mean that the Club has accepted the zines as 'a good thing', which is a pity – as the editors insist, "We are NOT the 'enemy within.'" One thing you can 'thank' *RI* for is the *Man Utd Magazine*, a spectacularly ill-judged attempt to muscle in on the fanzine market which was forced to relocate its position and become a newsagent read after the zines outsold it ten-to-one outside the ground. Street credibility cannot be bought by good production values and star co-op-eration.

Greater significance is often allocated to fanzines in general, especially by academics. A simplistic historical line has been drawn that sees the hooligan era being replaced post-Heysel by the fanzines, fuelled by Madchester-inspired love-ins and mass consumption of cannabis. Veg finds this a bit too pat;

49

violence was killed primarily by increased police efficiency, not by drug-crazed fans getting together singing 'One Love'. Moreover, in the midst of Madchester, it was still spectacularly easy to get your head kicked in on a Saturday night! Violence did indeed become 'unfashionable', especially when peripheral trouble-makers were getting nicked as well as the hard-core – after that, many just didn't fancy it any more. Veg remarks on how at Euro aways, the younger elements who were potentially 'up for it' were discouraged by older followers who would tell the teens to "put up or shut up" which invariably ended any prospective incidents.

Hillsborough was, of course, the death-knell for aggro; although the disaster was caused by poor police crowd-control, crowd misbehaviour had played its part outside the ground and the lesson was not lost on fans in general. The disaster cemented the post-Heysel process in which fans turned away from violence and towards new methods of maintaining tribal rivalries. It seems that fan groups now use 'intellectual' means rather than physical force in these conflicts – now the debate is about who has the most effective chants, the best singers, the most cutting lines of argument and the cruellest jokes rather than simply who can beat up whom. In such an environment, the role of the fanzine becomes clear and crucial: the zines have replaced the fighting crews as the vehicles of inter-fan conflict. They are the new rallying points and, in some senses, the new leaders. We should be grateful that in *Red Issue* we have the most vibrant, cutting and self-confident fanzine of them all.

Elsewhere in 88/89

- ❏ Rangers are in trouble again as Terry Butcher is done for kicking in a ref's door. Spotted a pattern here yet readers?
- ❏ The Hillsborough Disaster claims 96 lives. No comment necessary.

◻ Celtic beat Rangers in Cup Final. Several Rangers players cry openly. What a bunch of girls.

◻ Fourteen Liverpool fans are found guilty of Heysel manslaughter but are allowed to go home pending appeal. So much for Belgian justice – how many do YOU think returned to do time?!

◻ Don Revie dies of motor neurone disease. For some reason, the FA don't order a nationwide minute's silence.

◻ Arsenal, possibly for the first time ever, delight the nation by winning the title at Anfield. The Kop, aware of the TV cameras' presence, applaud the Londoners in a prime display of SMAC. Puke.

◻ The three Wallace brothers make history by appearing in the same 11 for the Saints; all very confusing for commentators and, one presumes, watching United scouts...

◻ The Stone Roses release their debut album; within two years, Manchester is full of Southern students waving Madchester editions of *The Face* trying to find the Haç. Thanks boys.

◻ French transfer of the year: Eric Cantona signs for Marseille.

1989/90

July 26, 1989; a day of infamy whose fifth anniversary passed unnoticed this year – the day Norm was sold to Everton. Losing McGrath and Strachan had been heart-rending enough but although Norm was the only one of this illustrious trio who failed to make an enduring impact elsewhere, he was the Red hero whose departure, surely, was the most keenly mourned. 'Tragedy' is a word rarely used with respect in football but the decline of Norman Whiteside deserves that appellation. When he popped up on 'Standing Room Only' last season, you couldn't help but grieve for the loss of his services to both United and football; the man is still younger than several current Premiership stars and should have been at the peak of his career, lifting titles in a Red shirt and captaining the Ulstermen in the World Cup.

Instead, he's now a student at Salford Uni with a developing lager paunch to match. Why did it have to be him? – couldn't the Lord have taken Mickey Phelan in his place? The old and increasingly tiresome debate about why Norm had to leave OT doesn't need to be rehashed here; Whiteside himself clearly wasn't blameless and we were perhaps unfair solely to lambast Fergie for the decision to sell. Nevertheless, it seemed too much of a coincidence that the last three Atkinson Boys – bar Robbo, of course – had all been disposed of by the kick-off of '89/'90; there had been a sense of inevitability about the fate of this trio for over 12 months. The fact that all three caught fire at their new clubs and had top seasons hardly improved our temper; their sales instilled in us a resentful grudge against Fergie that simmered below the surface and exploded later in the year. Maybe Alex was right to argue that the change did them good, that they wouldn't have produced the goods had they stayed on – but in the grim winter months ahead, few of us were particularly receptive to that line of spin-doctoring.

Still, at least for once we were going to get some funds for a shopping expedition to 'replace' these lost heroes. We didn't yet know the reason why but the Board had agreed to loosen the reins on Alex as a 'reward' for his sensible dealings so far (!) and Alex was soon out and about, waving the Edwards Gold Card at everything that moved – and at some that didn't, like Neil Webb. Admittedly, Webb seemed a good buy at the time, despite the rip-off price-tag that accompanies everything from the House of Clough. Mickey Phelan, by contrast, scarcely filled our hearts with joy; from the off, many of us saw him as yet another typical Fergie foster-child, a hard-running worker of no fixed talent perfectly equipped to join the Wimblearse set-up that Fergie appeared to be constructing.

One spot remained to be filled – a successor to McGrath. Glenn Hysen was earmarked for purchase but a combination of greed, Scouse sharp practice and United's parsimony saw him end up at Anfield. At the time, we viewed this as a shameful loss of face for United, a source of glee for the Scousers and another illustration of our transfer market ineptitude as formerly exemplified by the loss of Barnes and Gazza.

Of course, much to our delight, this Scandinavian drittsek erupted in Liverpool's faces; Hysen turned out to be the originator of a new Anfield tradition viz. the seasonal multi-million purchases of utterly useless defenders. (Hello there Stig, Mark, Razor and friends.) The failure of United to sign him had the most wonderful of pay-offs for us; Alex was forced to go in for Gary Pallister at the end of August. Boro scalped us for a record £2.3 million much to the amusement of our rivals but the last laugh has most certainly been on them. On such strokes of luck are championships won – it was the first turning point of an epochal season stuffed with moments of knife-edge crisis and lucky breaks, moments whose importance was only gradually appreciated as the months ground on.

* * * * *

In the days before the new season opened with the visit of the champions Arsenal to OT, we learned why we were suddenly so flush with loot to spend; Martin was gate-happy – he'd agreed to sell the club. The deliverance for which so many had prayed had come; Edwards would relinquish control to a moustachioed puff-ball non-entity called Michael Knighton who'd promised to inject millions and build a new Strettie. The delirium into which this astonishing news had transported us at first overwhelmed our critical faculties. So what if no one knew who this pretender to the throne was? So what if Edwards would still be lingering on at OT for three years like a fart in a phone booth? So what if the new guy, judging from his on-pitch, ball-juggling antics, was apparently a naff knobhead of the first degree? If it meant that the Wicked Witch of Wilmslow was gone, who cared who Dorothy was?

Robert Maxwell cared, for one. His papers did what Old Trafford should have done thoroughly before announcing their *fait accompli* to a hostile world. The journos checked out MK Holdings and the rest of Knighton's affairs, promptly discovering that the would-be Emperor had no clothes – and no bulging wallet either. Over 55 excruciating days, the entire horrendous mess played out as a mélange of Grand Guignol and Brian Rix farce all over the front pages; by the end of the performance, no trousers remained unlowered, no hairy bum unexposed. Edwards and Knighton had succeeded in making complete arses of both themselves and the Club to no avail whatsoever beyond Knighton getting a seat on the Board.

Apparently, this directorship was offered to convince Knighton to tear up the contract and get all those involved off the genital-impaling hook they'd devised for themselves. That the affair demonstrated the utter incompetence of certain individuals was obvious; the rest of the Board, particularly Charlton and Busby, were hugely unimpressed and the fans, when we'd stopped cringing in embarrassment, were both livid at the farrago we'd been put through and disappointed that we hadn't got rid of Edwards. Who can tell how much the team were affected? – it could hardly have helped.

The Chairman's personal standing with the faithful slipped into the slime of an all-time low; not only had he twice in five years sought to rid himself of the Club, but on both occasions he'd almost let us slide into the grasp of such loathable characters as Maxwell and Knighton. From that moment on, a stock exchange flotation became increasingly inevitable; Edwards was clearly determined to liquidise his shareholdings and a general sale was obviously going to be the only 'safe' way to let him do it. Bobby Charlton immediately proposed such a move which would allow fans to invest and thus take over – sadly, the eventual share-sale was apparently designed to exclude us and maximise the yields for Edwards. We were fools for believing that it could ever have been otherwise.

If we needed further evidence that OT was becoming a cess-pit full of broken promises and Mammon-worshipping grubbery, the publication that year of Smith & Crick's *'Betrayal of a Legend'* provided in it spades. David Smith was known by us all as the former supporters' chairman; Michael Crick, an ex-MGS boy now at 'Newsnight', is a doughty reporter and hard-core Red who'd become alarmed at the institutional failure at United. The book was a devastating account of the chicanery behind the scenes at the Club, thoroughly researched, forensically detailed and damning in conclusion. The picture it painted of the Edwards family was not a pretty one but it has never been legally challenged by those the authors attack, suggesting that you can rely on its veracity. It was certainly essential reading for all those who were not admirers of Edwards & Co and its emergence at that moment was perfectly timed. Its glum, foreboding final summary chimed smartly with the spirit of the times; was there ever a darker period since promotion than those last months of the '80s?

On that glorious, sun-drenched opening day, no one could have suspected what was to come. We demolished the champions in the second-half, winning 4-1 with a performance illuminated by a fabulous Webb strike on his debut. Delicious.

However, by the end of the month, we were back in familiar territory; fans getting treated like cattle on away days, the team playing like a Sexton side and mid-table trundlers making monkeys of us. At Palace, kick-off was delayed to let 2,000 Reds enter an all-ticket game cut-price as if Hillsboro' had never happened. Four days later, the usual chaos ensued at the Baseball Ground with the police and the club doing their best to provoke the terrace strife by completely cocking-up everything they did. Segregation and crowd control were obviously alien concepts to the ground authorities there who'd learned nothing from earlier visits from the Reds. Naturally, Derby proceeded to outplay us, as did Norwich at OT the following Wednesday night. Pally made his debut, played well and then gave away a penalty thus establishing his early pattern from the start of his OT career. Leighton also started as he meant to go on, adding another blunder to his impressive collection at Derby. The team as a whole, perhaps understandably, were playing like strangers. Clearly, there was some serious gelling to be done if this new team was to survive.

As the Knighton fiasco raged on, Paul Ince and Danny Wallace arrived from the south, Incey having survived 11th hour hitches and mortally offended every Hammer in the process – nice one. Wallace, apparently, was supposed to provide the width we got from Strachan but ended up providing what we got from Milne more often than not. Fergie had splashed millions on five new guys of whom only two were truly to make United grade. It was the month that 'Fools Gold' came out – how apt.

We lost at Goodison, (where some Reds showed Edwards-style PR skills by singing 'Hillsboro 89') making it three defeats in a row. True, we hammered Millwall 5-1 with Hughesy getting a hat-trick featuring a pulsating opener but the game was merely a glint of sunlight in the midst of a thunderstorm. The following week was our return to Maine Road.

* * * * *

A Blue baby is born in a Moss Side gutter. At the age of three, it finally manages to say its first words. As his beaming, beflared Bluenose father looks on, the little urchin burbles the Maine Road Mantra...'5-1, 5-1'.

I was tempted not to write anything about that Black September day but my psychiatrist reckons it's a good thing to confront trauma. In any event, much of it has conveniently receded from memory, apart from the mighty punch-up in the stands. Some years later, I met a Blue ringleader in one of Her Majesty's establishments – the natural and inevitable destination for so many on the Kippax – who admitted that too many of his cohorts had bottled out of it that day; his glee at the result was thus tempered by the shame of terrace defeat. It is, of course, doubly amusing that the only memory of the match for the country at large is Hughesy's wondrous strike. Even in triumph, there is bitterness for our backward Blue cousins.

But hey, let's be magnanimous. Well done City – for once you managed to beat us. Cling to it forever if you must; I guess the wretched must take their consolation wherever they can find it. I suppose it's understandable that something so rare should be celebrated for an eternity. For us, there's less need for years of crowing over particular results since we have a seemingly inexhaustible supply of City-thumpings on which to draw. Yet there is something rather sad and pathetic in hearing a Bitterman five years after the event, still harking back to his sole moment of temporary ascendancy as if it were somehow still relevant. If the derby reverse had been truly significant, perhaps akin to our twin triumphs of '76/'77 which cost City the title, then maybe such tedious repetition would be justified. Otherwise a derby win is only valid until the next encounter. If it had wrecked the team psychologically for months afterwards, fair enough, gloat 'till your face turns as purple as your disgusting away kit. But United ended the season with glory at Wembley, the first steps to the Valhalla of '93, whereas City, as usual, ended up with more moths in the Trophy Room.

The truth is that the 5-1 farrago was simply a freakish

absurdity, a day when quantum physics did its worst, even more unlikely than lightning striking twice, or City holding silver in their oft-fingerprinted paws. It had no significance, no after effects and thus no real purpose or meaning. One looks back and marvels at the ridiculousness of the whole day, an afternoon when God took pity on the poor hovel-dwellers and decided to give them a few days of ecstasy before they subsided back into their customary misery. What is so pitiful is that even now, the Blue vocabulary remains so dominated by two numbers. Don't they yet realise that every time they summon up the spirits of that dead day, they draw attention once again to the fact that they have had nothing since to celebrate? In a way, the cry of '5-1' is as potent a condemnation of City's mediocrity as '18 years and won f*ck all'. May the bedraggled Bluenoses continue to intone this doleful reminder of isolated glory as long as they like; we should, metaphorically, pat the poor souls on the head and leave them to reminisce in the twilight of their Moss Side mausoleum.

* * * * *

Winter approached, the nights grew darker; United got worse and the knives were getting sharpened. Of course, there were still odd moments of iridescence when some of the team's donkeys managed a good game and the team showed their potential; the wins at Coventry and Luton were sporadically fabulous – Blackmore playing well, Phelan scoring, McClair looking dangerous. These were not common sights at the time. What we *were* getting used to was watching United slip slowly down the toilet as the New Year hove into view. Some of those games featured team performances that weren't just completely turd-like – they were the brown encrustations at the bottom of the U-bend. Possibly the worst was the game against Spurs at home; humiliated three-nil, we jeered them off the pitch and vented our rage at the manager and chairman.

The 'Fergie Out' campaign had begun in earnest, seemingly started by a bloke in J-Stand who just couldn't take anymore and rapidly taken up by K-Stand and the rest; banners began to appear and 'Fergie Out' hit the top of the terrace hit parade. The defeat at Charlton, in many ways a new low even in this season, cemented our view; we might as well admit it – most of us wanted Alex out. If the rest of the stadium needed further convincing, December did the job. Not a win in seven games; we failed to beat any of the four London sides we faced in consecutive games; Fergie dropped Hughes for the Palace game and we lost it.

That match seemed to symbolise the malaise we were in. Mystifying selection by a manager who'd bought a load of expensive parts for a machine that he had no idea how to assemble. Dropping the only class performer of the time whilst leaving the ham-actors in place. Resorting to five at the back and an attacking policy of up-field punts for out-of-synch forwards. Losing to horrible second-rate suburban joke-clubs like Crystal Palace. It was all there that day. Even the one good performance of the month, typically at Anfield, was disappointing; we hadn't got the win we deserved and Robbo had been injured. Merry F*cking Christmas.

By New Year's Day – and yet another incredibly tedious nil-nil at home – Alex's blood was in the water and the tabloid sharks were racing in for the feeding frenzy. United had been drawn away to Forest, our bogeyist of bogey teams, in the FA Cup. We had six injuries, the game was live on BBC1 and we hadn't won a match for two months. The fixture screamed 'catastrophe'; our season threatened to end on January 7th, with only a relegation battle ahead. Hacks tripped over themselves to be the most condemnatory of Fergie's record, a competition probably won by Brian Glanville who authoritatively damned Alex's entire period as an unmitigated disaster. Reading this stuff, you couldn't help but feel Fergie's managerial life expectancy could now be measured in days. The sense of the time was that a knock-out by Forest would release the Edwards butcher's chopper. Now, of course, everyone claims that there was never such a possibility, that the Cup run didn't save Fergie's career and that the Board would have stood by him throughout. Pardon us for not swallowing that one whole.

It's at times like this you realise that when you become a football fan, you check in any sense of logical reason at the door. An objective analyst would have prescribed a boycott of that Cup game, a defeat for United and, presumably, the dismissal of Fergie would have followed. Instead we turned up in our thousands at the City Ground, gave the greatest display of fevered Red-worship seen that season and inspired our make-shift team to a gritty, backs-to-the-wall 1-0 win. Robins got the goal that was to lead him and the team to Wembley but the assist should surely be credited to the travelling Reds.

The victory was akin to the lancing of an enormous botty boil; a gigantic wave of relief seemed to sweep through the club. Despite our continued poor league form – a win at the Den was required a month later to prevent us dropping into the bottom three – no match ever held quite the same sense of impending doom again. True, the team continued to produce offal for the majority of the rest of the season. True, Fergie, as far as we were concerned, was on probation for the next six months. Yet as long as the Cup run continued, there remained visible the faintest of flickering lights at the end of the tunnel – the floodlights of Wembley on a Thursday night in May.

There's not much point in dwelling on the rest of the league programme. United avoided relegation – that's it really. A run of four League wins after Easter around the time of the semi-finals saw to that, Mark Robins coming off the bench to score in each of them. Everton Reserves City, who'd become twice as old and twice as Scouse under the tutelage of their 'saviour' Howard Kendall, grabbed a spawny point at OT; Liverpool's Ronnie Whelan scored the most spectacular own goal we'd ever seen but had the last laugh as we lost 1-2. It was our first OT loss against the shell suits in eight seasons – our miserable display deserved little else. Everton took a point, too, in a game that saw Norm being booed on his return to OT, presumably by the same United Road and Strettie welcoming committee who aired the Hillsboro' chant for the other Mersey mongs. These were not our most glory-filled days. Our last awayday of the season at Forest typified our League year; a spineless showing, four conceded in 20 minutes and a team with their mind clearly on the Cup.

* * * * *

Of course, one reason for United's miserable League form was the absence of Robson, who made only 20 appearances. Like Martin Buchan before him, Robson's role as our leader, talisman, driving force and inspirational example was so crucial as to be devastating when we were deprived of him. At the end of Robbo's last 'full' season, '91/'92, he'd played 311 League games for United – but out of a possible total of 460 plus. He would habitually lose a dozen games a season, inevitably at vital periods and with title-blowing consequences. United had failed to win the title in 1977 because we'd fallen apart during Buchan's injury; this scenario was replicated half-a-dozen times during the '80s with Robbo. Imagine losing Eric for three months and you get some idea of the Robson Effect.

Actually, whilst you were under the bedclothes and away from prying ears, you could perhaps admit to yourself that we often used injuries to Buchan and Robson as excuses for our failure to win titles. At school, you might have convincingly argued that only their absences prevented the Reds from conquering all, but in private you knew that Liverpool's system could withstand the loss of a top player whereas ours could not. This isn't so terrible an admission in retrospect; in fact, it's one of the most heartening differences between us and the Anfield Machine (deceased).

To them, the collective is everything, their players being mere cogs in the apparatus who must never be allowed to get above themselves. But to us, the individual is all. We love our stars and don't care how glitter-drenched they allow themselves to become. So what if sometimes our whole is somewhat less than the sum of its parts? Far better to revel in the

61

memories of sunlit displays by Hill, Giggs or Hughes than fawn over the production line displays of a mechanical outfit of 'worthy' Scousers. What brings greater delight to the senses: Robson's solo heroics in '84 against Barca or 'Pool's efficiently dull team showing against Roma two months later?

Great United teams have always consisted of brilliant individuals who perform as a team with varying degrees of cohesion; Liverpool have relied on solid players who fit into the bigger picture. They would surely have been Stalin's favourite team. No wonder there are so many Militant supporters on the Kop. Maybe their ideology brought more routine success; yet I know what real freedom-loving football connoisseurs prefer to watch. The bitter truth for Scousers is that our one glorious, thrilling, against-the-odds Euro Cup win will always be more cherished and honoured than their four mainly drab, colourless and easy wins will ever be. That's why they hate and resent us so much; that is the difference between our way and theirs; that is why the world supports United and not Liverpool.

* * * * *

Ironically, this dreary diet of lumpen football and passionless, meaningless games was being served up to one of the best audiences we'd had for years. The United Road was making the most of its swansong months, especially excited by the re-appearance of their special friend Colin Gibson, whilst K-Stand had become, in a matter of 12 months or so, the new heart of Old Trafford. How quickly the K-Standers had become noted for their friendly greeting of away support, their cheery banter with Edwards and Fergie and their balanced appreciation of United's effort when they lost...Quite simply, K-Stand was the most feared seated section in England and by now the most vociferous vocal support we had.

Who knows why they'd emerged at this moment? Was it the influx of ex-Strettie boys from the late '70s or the first arrivals from the moribund Paddock? Whatever the sociology behind the K-Stand, we were grateful for its new pre-eminence – they, like the rest of us, deserved better then we were getting. Similarly, the away support was about to enter a new golden age. The Cup run rejuvenated the travelling army – the increased Cup success of the next few years meant more special awaydays with bigger ticket allocations and an ever-intensifying support. The latter part of the season was like '78/'79 revisited – a struggling team who seemed to have lost the plot somehow getting to Wembley on a tide of fervent fans and bare-knuckled determination on the pitch. *'Onward Fergie's Soldiers'* anyone?

One of the great football clichés is that any faintly good story gets tagged 'Roy of the Rovers stuff' by the tabloids but in United's case this season, the tag was apt. Drawn away for every single tie at tricky grounds against awkward opposition, constantly bedevilled by injuries and under intensive media scrutiny, it was a remarkable achievement for such a mediocre team. For every improving player such as Pally, Bruce and Ince we had a corresponding liability to contend with like Leighton, Phelan or Anderson.

We'd given Mickey and his atrocious Hitlerian moustache a full season to impress us but we could bear no more. Every time Fergie praised his hard work 'covering every blade of grass on the pitch' (Cliché Alert!!) we cringed. A bloody lawn-mower 'covers every blade' but you don't want a Qualcast at number five do you? Though at least a lawn-mower wouldn't treat the ball as if it were a primed grenade to be disposed of as rapidly as possible. Leighton was far more serious a case. By now, he was openly reviled by us all. *Red Issue* were leading a full-blown campaign to get him dumped, releasing a hugely successful T-shirt featuring the Leighton Condom design. Alex, however, pretended not to hear our cat-calls during warm-ups and even in April was still lauding Jim as the best goalie in Scotland – as if that would make us feel any better every time our hearts froze when a cross came into Leighton's view.

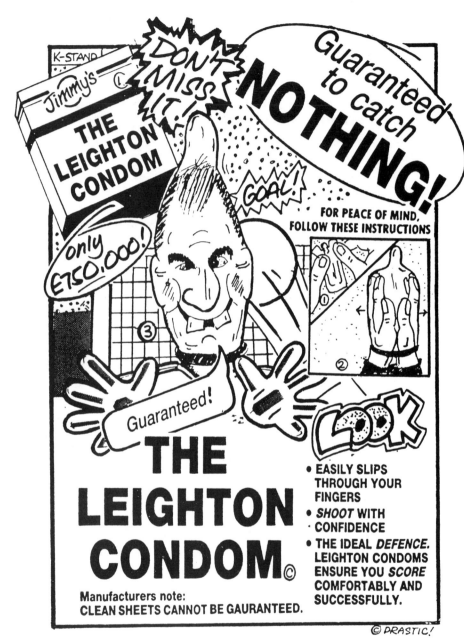

64

Still, recalling Roy of the Rovers again, we had one genuine hero – a true life incarnation of 'Stark – Match Winner For Hire' which you might remember from the comic – Mark Robins. After he was sold to Norwich, Fergie said that Robins "was not a Man United player", implying that there was something about him that made him unsuitable for a true Fergie United team. Dead right – he was a young, local lad and proven deadly goalscorer of great consistency. Obviously not a proper United player – what were we thinking of? Give us strikers of the calibre of Brazil and Davenport any day, Mr Manager. Good grief...Back in 89/90, Robins became a talismanic player, as vital to our Cup success and to keeping Fergie off the dole queue as anyone else. Once again, it was youth to the rescue which made our triumph all the more sweet.

At Hereford, on a sodden bog against typical lower-division clatterers, Clayton Blackmore answered the call with a late winner that allowed us to forget his early season sins for a while. At St. James Park, in the midst of a hurricane, Robins again allowed us to seize the initiative. In a thrilling game that shortened our life spans, we won 3-2 and marvelled at a couple of rarities – a good Wallace game'n'goal and McClair's first strike for 17 games (which, of course, he almost missed). Even though we'd got through to a quarter-final at Bramhall Lane, no one was revelling in Cup Fever yet. The lessons of the previous two seasons had been learned; besides, our League form was still so poor that no one could have much confidence on 'skill' getting us through. This was to be a Cup won not on brilliant play or mercurial talent but through sheer bloody-minded determination, driving us from the brinks of precipices to chain-smoking, one-goal victories.

Choccy got the only goal against the Blades in front of a magnificent Red force who now, at last, could begin to dream of Wembley one more. 1985 seemed an eon away – the players long gone, the style long-lost – we'd been through so much upheaval and upset since then. We could only hope that someone disposed of Liverpool, that we could struggle our way to the Cup and pray that our success would prove to be some sort of turning point. Oldham, the nation's favourite plucky underdogs, stood in our way. Piling into what appeared to be some sort of unsegregated Maine Road – in fact, we'd somehow managed to end up outnumbering the opposition as usual – we witnessed the most ridiculously dramatic game of the year. Leighton's cock-up, Robbo and Webb back from injury and turning it on, Wallace coming off the bench to score, a cert penalty denied and Roger Palmer, not for the first time, breaking our hearts with a late equaliser.

We'd seen a classic match and gave the Latics due credit despite their support's complete lack of vocal originality – 'Come on Oldham' really *is* their only song. In the replay, Andy Ritchie reminded us of one of Dave Sexton's worst selling decisions before, inevitably, Robins got on to Phelan's pass and slotted it home with ice-cool aplomb. Even Barry Davies was excited. We were, of course, ecstatic – at Wembley once more, the last place any of us expected to see again back in mid-winter.

The run-up to a United Cup Final has its usual special traditions that you can rely on; City will kiss-up disgustingly to whoever we're playing, there'll be a tabloid story on Martin Edwards and the opposition chairman will whinge pathetically about the ticket allocation. City and Palace duly held their love-in which at least had the pleasant by-product of bringing Charlton Athletic and United together. United's favourite tabloid the *Sunday People* – part of the Maxwell empire that hadn't forgiven us for failing to succumb to the fat crook's advances – ran a wonderful piece on an alleged relationship between Edwards and a newsreader of minor repute. None of us believed it, of course, especially not *Red Issue*...Ron Noades, Palace chairman and race relations specialist, had the unbelievable chutzpah to moan about the lack of tickets for his glory-hunting supporters (average gate '88/'89: 10,500). Everyone hooted in derision at him, of course, which didn't prevent Chelsea from making similar arses of themselves in '94.

DHSS ENTERPRISES AND **WEMBLEY STADIUM LTD**
present

ALEX AID

Wembley Stadium
Saturday 12th May

13 of the Worlds top footballers try to keep Fergie out of the dole queue by winning the F A Cup

starring

*Mark HUGHES * Bryan ROBSON*
Neil WEBB Paul INCE*

plus full supporting cast

SPECIAL FEATURE!!

Backing Vocals will be provided by the infamous RED ARMY, performing all their greatest hits . . . .
"PRIDE OF ALL EUROPE"
"GLORY, GLORY, MAN. UNITED"
"IF YOU ALL HATE SCOUSERS...."
and the all-time dancefloor classic ...
"...LETS ALL 'AVE A DISCO" -

should any of the main stars fail to perform, MARK ROBINS will save the day!

TICKETS FOR THIS EVENT ARE ONLY AVAILABLE FROM BOBBY CHARLTON ENTERPRIZES AT A COST OF £150 EACH. (PAYABLE IN ADVANCE, USED £5 + £10 NOTES ONLY!)

Supposedly the first Final match made great TV but for Reds it was purgatory on earth. Jim Leighton excelled himself, letting in two soft goals and injecting a fatal lack of confidence into the entire defence that made us fear for our lives every time the ball ballooned over towards our area. We'd dominated huge chunks of the game but were still only 2-1 up when Ian Wright came on. Yet again, a black sub had come on to sink us. Not for the last time, Hughesy saved the season with a late Wembley equaliser. For all of us, it was torture; we laid the blame squarely at the door of Fergie & Jim who now appeared to us to be father and son. What other explanation could there be for persisting with the hapless Scot?

The rest is legend. On Thursday night, many Reds were unaware until the teams emerged from the tunnel that Leighton had, at last, been axed. Les Sealey who, as the more pessimistic reminded us, had once cost Luton a Cup, was on in his place. Within five minutes, Les had stamped his authority on the box and from then on in, Palace never looked like scoring. Apparently, Jim's shock omission had completely wrecked their tactical plans and they were forced to revert to type – that is, attempting to kick every Red shirt off the pitch.

Any sympathy they had garnered on the Saturday was lost along with any chance of winning. We stayed cool, played our way through the minefield carefully and revelled in the justice of Lee Martin's net-billowing winner. How fitting that the final act of salvation was perpetrated by one of Fergie's Fledglings; how cruel that Lee, like the rest of his class of '89, was blighted by injury in the most crucial years. The Cup was ours – the most improbable result from the most turbulent of seasons. Little did we know that this was only the first showering of silver from a cascade to come. Things can only get better? Right, this time.

Elsewhere in 89/90

◻ Ibrox bigots are horrified when Catholic Mo Johnston signs; their pathetic reaction reminds the nation that Rangers stink.

◻ The Taylor Report is published sounding the death-knell for the terraces. Thank you South Yorkshire police.

◻ Sourness breaches a touchline ban and picks up a record fine, his second offence of this sort. Were the Anfield board simply asleep in these years?

◻ 5,000 Leeds fans, only half with tickets, travel to Bournemouth to clinch promotion. They 'celebrate' with a riot throughout the sleepy town, leading to 123 arrests. Charming boys.

◻ The Germans are the least popular, least glorious and least entertaining winners of the worst World Cup ever – but at least the Argies don't win it.

◻ City manage to finish even lower in the league than us and get knocked out of the Cup at the first hurdle by mighty Millwall. Liverpool win their last ever title, we hope.

◻ The United Road Paddock is seated during the summer to become the unloved North Stand Lower; a little bit more of OT dies. Colin Gibson denies responsibility.

◻ United get the go ahead to enter the European Cup Winners Cup in 1990/91, leading the nation back into Europe like we did in 1956.

◻ Marseilles loan Eric Cantona to Montpellier who are promptly inspired to a French Cup Final win.

1990/91

Once upon a time, United's forlorn title challenges used to follow an almost comforting tradition. We'd get involved in a two or three horse race, reach the final furlong and then finish fourth, having been distracted by the gleam of some tempting Cup silverware. Under Fergie, it seemed, League failure was to be achieved far more efficiently; by November, our title hopes would already be dashed completely. No need to raise your expectations when Adolph, Fatboy and Co. were there to smash your dreams up right from the off.

When the Red Army reassembled in August, there were two changes to digest. Firstly, the United Road boys had been forced to find a new home and were duly welcomed to apply for Library tickets in the Strettie. This injection of pure nuttery revitalised the slumbering end, helping to make the last two years in the heart of Old Trafford memorable seasons. Secondly, Denis Irwin, who'd impressed in Oldham's Cup runs of 1990, had arrived to fill the problem fullback spot. Not all of us took to him instantly; a hard-core remained unconvinced until well into '91/'92, moaning about his susceptibility to pace and his general anonymity. Spotting his resemblance to cartoon hero Mr Benn, some wished that when Denis went into the dressing room, he too could disappear to a magic world – permanently. It's been a pleasure to be proved wrong.

Some things never change, however, one being that United will never get a break in a game refereed by George Courtney – we were forced to settle for a share in the Charity Shield against the Anfield alley-lurkers. Four weeks later, the same opposition provided our season's nadir in a stupid, ridiculous game – how can anyone play so brightly yet go three down before you'd eaten your second pie? The lack of fight from United in the second half though was disgusting to behold; spineless second halves were a common feature of those first few months.

The fact is that until December, United were playing as if Wembley had never happened. Too many individual players were still not at their peak, like Pally and Ince, whilst others such as Webb and Phelan were on their way to being enrolled into the Milne Hall of Shame. However, Clayton was at least having his best-ever season, causing many of us to consume barrel-loads of humble-pie and even Danny Wallace managed a good month in November. But in general, we were witnessing Fergie's Wimblearse Part Two – predictable moves, offside and five-at-the-back and the usual deathless, sub-'O' level tactics.

The League Cup tie against the mighty and fearsome Halifax epitomised the Man U malaise: halfway through the home leg, two up, yet playing half-a-dozen in defence thus reducing OT to a completely comotose condition. The home defeats by Forest and Arsenal were particularly dire – we seemed to be a team going absolutely nowhere in true Sextonian-style. Not even the early Euro rounds could lift us, drawn as we were against two less-than-thrilling prospects in Pecsi and Wrexham. Even then, the team managed only to fuel our discontent, the performances against a ninth-rate Munkas being particularly woesome.

October's visit from the Gooners brought the usual display of grim percentage football from the unloved-Champions-to-be but was enlivened by a tremendously enjoyable punch-up that, unfortunately, enraged the FA. Limpar and Denis Irwin provided the unlikeliest sparks but Choccy and the chinless wonder Winterburn were soon eagerly renewing old acquaintances from '89 heavily supported by 17 other players...The Clubs ended up being done for 'bringing the game into disrepute', surely the least appropriate of grounds. Can you think of anything that would do more good for football attendances than the prospect of a regular 20-man fist-fight? Let's face it, the scrap was the only thing from that match that any of us remember. Perhaps Sky TV missed a trick here – what about half-time fights between selected players? Keane v McMahon over six rounds anyone?

Of course, there were some highlights amidst the lowlife. Robin's brace against QPR included a lovely chip – not a Man U player, remember – and the Palace win provided signs of a team starting to coalesce into something less excremental. There was the delight of the League Cup KO of the work-shy Murkey-siders and the joyous relief that Choccy's pair against the Bitters at Maine Road brought to those who hadn't left with 10 minutes to go. But even in 'triumph' such as escaping 3-3 in the derby, there was despair – what on earth was going on when Scouse rejects like City could threaten to humiliate us for a second year running? We'd got a snide little point, scarcely deserved – great fun at the time and a source of intense bitterness for the Bluenoses but hardly a good portent for our team generally.

By November 25th and our third home defeat against Chelsea, it was obvious we weren't going to win the League. But the season and the team were to be saved, with the inspiration coming from the most unlikely of sources for United.

* * * * *

Some of the season's most orgasmic moments had been provided by that runt of a competition, the League Cup, a tournament so lacking in class that we hadn't bothered to play in it until a narked Alan Hardaker made us. You often felt that we just weren't arsed enough about this tin pot and that consequently we would win it at will if we ever put our backs into it. Thus it was in 1991: a dazzling run featuring some classic United performances over hated rivals as if to say – 'this is what happens when we try, mortals.' Three clashes stand out: the Sheep semi, the Granny Stabbers at home and the so-called 'mighty' Arsenal away. All were won in such a cocky fashion as to plunge our opponents into City-like bitterness for months afterwards; it makes it all the more aggravating that the run was to end in such anticlimax.

Lee Sharpe was playing with the insatiable hunger and vigour of a beginner; he was like the monkey who'd just learned to masturbate. He excelled himself against the Arse with a hat-trick of epic proportions, including a sublime curler from 20 yards that was undoubtedly the best piece of football Highbury had seen since the Reds were last in town. There was some sort of madness in the air that night. Even Danny Wallace had a good game. After all, Arsenal were the League's most formidable side, in the middle of a Championship season during which they would lose only one match. Yet we slaughtered them 6-2, their heaviest home defeat in 40 years, a match whose mere mention is guaranteed to silence any lippy Gooner. It wasn't as if they played especially badly; at one point they'd made it 3-2 hadn't they? It was the brilliance of *our* play, not the failings of theirs that produced the victory. It was a sign of what was around the corner – *La Gloire* as Eric and Napoleon might say.

"Champions" Liverpool were swept aside 3-1 at OT. The two allegedly greatest teams in England had been shown to be worthless and helpless against an in-form United side. 'Twas ever thus, Horatio': how used we are to seeing United humiliate supposed superiors before succumbing to the division's detritus. At least until 1993 anyway. Hughes studded the game with a goal fit for the stars – a long range effort with such a gorgeous parabola that, as it screamed into the net over Grob's flailing fingers, seemed to shout 'Cop that, Bruce you clown.' Sweet revenge for the earlier League reverse indeed.

The semi was even crueller. The Sheep strained every farm-built muscle in their woolly bodies, played well enough to beat any other team but still couldn't do us. Sharpe roasted Sterland to such a crisp that he was never taken seriously again. Watching Lee brought back happy memories of Hill and Coppell against the Sheep in '77 creating yet another disastrous semi set-back for the Tykes. How they must loathe us. Ha!

* * * * *

RED-EYE

"That Sunday, away to Leeds, I had been unable to get tickets for the United end, so I got tickets for an executive suite called The Captains Lounge. For the first time ever, I had to go to a football game in a suit and tie. As we got to the ground, there was already a lot of tension and aggro an hour before the kick off, so it was with a degree of relief that we entered the stadium unmolested.

The Captains Lounge was (is?) a lounge/bar area through which you pass before going up a stairway to your seats. The block of seats attached to the lounge are located high up in the corner of the stadium, and, here's the good bit, next to and overlooking the kop.

Of the 200 or so people in our block, maybe half were Reds, and we sung ourselves hoarse for the next 90 minutes, mainly because of the constant Munich chants from the kop, aimed at us, maybe because we were intruders in their part of the ground. Again and again, venomously: "Who's that lying on the runway..........'cos they can't get their aeroplane to go!" The bastards!!

And then Lee Sharpe scored!

The elation, the ecstasy, the JOY! We went bananas! The morons on the kop replied with a shower of coins hurled at us, and a charge at us which the police stopped with drawn truncheons. For some reason it did not matter. I wasn't scared, as I thought I would be, just way, way over the moon. That last minute goal released the tension in us and the hate in them that had been building up throughout the match. It just did not matter. We were going to Wembley, and those bastards weren't.

The final whistle went. The police hustled us out of our seats, into the lounge and locked us in (or, to be more accurate, locked the kop out). There was a fight in the lounge (half of those there were Leeds fans), bricks were thrown through the windows from outside. Tension was very high.

Gradually, things calmed down. Manchester fans were asked to stay in the lounge whilst those from Leeds told to go. Finally, about half an hour after full time, we were taken back to our seats and then marched around the pitch perimeter to the bulk of United fans at the far end of the ground. Twenty minutes later, we were allowed out and headed home.

For Lee Sharpe, it was probably a goal he might or might not remember.

For all the United fans there, it was a tremendous result that saw us on our way to Wembley.

But for ME, it was probably the most special moment in 22 years of watching United. I'll probably never go back to Elland Road, because it could only be an anti-climax, but for as long as I live I will never forget the split second of stunned silence that greeted Sharpe's goal, nor the sheer joy that followed it."

Philip Ellis, Whitefield

"As we approached Elland Road it became obvious the Leeds Neanderthals were spoiling for a fight. A number of them mingled in with the scant police escort and with shouts of 'Come on Munich', tried to goad United fans into a fight. When we finally got to the area behind the away seating, the already sparse police escort became non-existent for those who had seats in the South Stand. The 70 yard walk to the seats entrance saw many United fans the victims of attacks by the Yorkshire scum.

As we celebrated at the end, Leeds were falling over themselves in an effort to invade the pitch and attack our players, officials and supporters in the corner nearest the Main Stand. We later heard they'd attacked our team coach and the management of Montpellier who'd come to watch us.

Meanwhile those United fans who had stood on the Lowfields Road were moved to a pen behind the terracing, an act of pure stupidity by Yorkshire's finest as the scum on the outside showered our fans with various missiles. It was a full 20 minutes before the plod had the brains to move the United contingent.

Elsewhere Leeds fans were in the midst of a pitched battle with police behind the South Stand as they attempted to gain entry to United's seats and smashed car windscreens and headlamps in the car park of the pub behind that stamp. It took 50 minutes to clear the area so that we could be let out. 22 out of the 23 arrested were Leeds fans but it seems facts are not allowed to clear the smokescreen that Leeds and the police create in an effort to deflect blame or their disgracefully behaved fans and the inefficient boys in blue."

Red Issue Vol 3 Ish.9 April 1991

© DRASTIC

Chief Super. David Clarkson:

"The problem was caused when gesturing United fans provoked Leeds supporters in the north-west seated corner. Unfortunately the Leeds supporters responded. You can't control every pub from here to Manchester (?). Normally we have no problems at this ground."

– Oh well, that's all right then isn't it!

⌐ eeds police chief quoted in Daily Star Feb 25th 1991)

* * * * *

And so to Wembley. If there had been any logic or justice in it, our final opponents should've been City or Everton so as to complete this glorious run. But no, we were given Second Division Sheffield Wednesday, which should've been sufficient to ring the alarms in our souls. They were managed by fat Scouse United reject 'Big Ron' which only made the result even more predictable – that, at least, we would be leaden; at most we would lose. As every child should know by now, United are only truly great against the most difficult opposition, especially in Finals. Give us lowly opponents and watch us flounder – Southampton in '76, the first games against Brighton and Palace in '83 and '90 and now the Owls – all featured United at their most nervously vulnerable. Pit us against Champions and favourites like the Scouse in '77 and '85 or Barca in '91 and we're in our element. It's typically United. What can you do?

Naturally, the following year United demonstrated another Red tradition, that of bouncing back from disappointment to make full amends the next time around, by beating Forest to lift the Washing Machine Cup at last. Sheridan's goal is all but forgotten and Sharpe's trio will live in the memory forever. The climax was awful but wasn't the foreplay great?!

* * * * *

77

It would be too pat to call the drubbing of Arsenal the turning point of the season – we didn't become a Eurochamp team overnight – but it felt at the time that this is what we could do if our dogs of war were let off the tactical leash. Key players had revelled in the free roles given to them. Who knows what made Fergie change tack that night but it proved everything we'd been saying: give the lads their heads and they'll happily smash in someone else's. That night also marked the full technicolour emergence of Lee Sharpe as a young, uninhibited winger, conjuring up reminiscences of the Docherty years. He was on his way to the PFA Award and his partnership with Hughesy was to bring Sparky eight goals in January and the senior PFA Award. This was what we called value for LMTB money indeed.

Two unbeaten months followed. The Sharpe shuffle was born at Goodison; erstwhile bogey team Norwich got comprehensively scalped on Boxing Day; Sharpey savaged Sunderland to create a 3-0 win; Hughesy concluded his record-breaking month with a fulminating hat-trick against the Saints and a match-winning volley of purest venom against the black pudding Wanderers in the Cup. At last, almost by accident, the team had begun to gell. The confidence that these months had engendered in the team set us up for the twin trophy assaults to come. Mouths watered – genitals tingled. This was more like it.

As United battled through their routes to Wembley and Rotterdam, League fixtures took on a secondary role which was largely understandable; only in a rough period after the Sheep semi when we lost four League games in a row did this Cup prioritisation become damaging and Alex was forced to remind the team of their obligation to perform for the OT regulars. The team sharpened up; Ince got his long-overdue first of the season at The Dell, Clayton chipped a cool one at the City ground and then, after the return from France, Bruce got five goals in the three wins on the trot. He was to end the year with 19 goals, a ridiculous number for a defender. But we all realised, and most accepted, that the League was there to keep the team ticking over in between the star games that studded the run-in – the European Cup Winners' Cup matches.

Nevertheless, we still finished a faintly respectable 6th, our final win coming in the OT-leg of the derby when a disgustingly young novice we'd pinched from the Blues scored his first Red goal – Ryan Giggs. City, incidentally, with no Cup Finals to occupy their minds, took advantage of our last eight dropped points to sneak in and finish 5th, prompting mass celebrations in the Moss Side gutters and proclamations that this was a "sign of things to come" – how sad for our success-starved Bluenose friends that their trivial triumph was soon to be utterly eclipsed in Holland.

* * * * *

What a pain it was to have to wait four months after the Wrexham Euro tie to resume our campaign. Presumably this delay is to allow various Europuffs to have their mid-winter breaks and then get back into the swing of things afterwards. Clearly a bit of snow and sub-zero temperature is too much for our continental confrères. No wonder they lose so many wars – and no wonder John Barnes was always so keen to play over there; no need for the thermal underwear when you're tucked up inside over Christmas.

To draw Montpellier in the quarter-finals was wonderful. The last opponents we wanted were either manky Mitteleuropa no-marks or crack-Euro giants over whom victories would be either inglorious certainties or highly improbable. Montpellier, with whom a certain Eric Cantona had won the French Cup in 1990, were third in the league, fairly glamorous and boasted an Italia '90 star in Carlos Valderamma. But best of all, the draw meant a spring jaunt to the south of France, to the edge of Provence when the air, sun and general ambience were at their seasonal peak. As we were to discover, the city itself is almost as beautiful as its environs and, happily for some of us, contains the most luscious French crumpet outside the Paris *seizième*.

First, however, we had to face them on our beach of a pitch at OT. The French seasiders must have felt quite at home; the surface was fit only for deckchairs, not top football. More worrisome was the trough of poor form we'd slunk into – we were bang in the centre of four straight losses and the tie could hardly have arrived at a worse moment. Our fears were confirmed within a quarter of an hour. Minutes after Choccy's 60 second goal, Lee Martin, the FA Cup winner, had put through the Strettie goal. A moment of pure mortification for all 42,000 of us and from then on, Montpellier out-thought us and got a deserved draw. Hughesy guaranteed himself a warm Provençal welcome by getting Baills sent off after executing a skilled Klinsmannism. The French were clearly delighted with the result as they swaggered off – their over-confidence was to be their undoing. We made all the right noises about getting a result over there, though few in the media bought this line. The nodding lapdogs in many a TV studio pronounced the match to be an exemplification of Euro guile outfoxing dim Anglo hoofers. But by the time of the return leg, our form had improved enough to give us confidence that we could pull it off.

The 'official' away support from the Club numbered 500 but on arrival found themselves swamped by brigades of the Red Army who'd made their own way down. The fabulous Place de la Comedie filled with Reds knocking back deceptively strong French lager; those still capable of remembering their 'O'-level French found the lithe young creatures in the student quarter five minutes stagger away surprisingly accommodating. This was turning out to be a dress-rehearsal for Rotterdam – the performance on the pitch was even more impressive. Clayton's 30-yard free-kick allowed us to play a classic Europan game-plan as we frustrated both their overpaid stars and belligerent support. Stevie Bruce made it 2-0 from the spot, Robbo blanked out Valderamma and United were through. We had played like Euro veterans, this from a Club making its first appearance in Euro competition for six years. The Stade de Mosson had been at its most intimidating but we had risen magnificently to the occasion in true Red style.

We deserved the stroke of luck we got in the semi-final draw. Avoiding Juve and Barca, we were sent to Warsaw to play Legia, conquerors of Sampdoria in the quarters. Robbo was suspended, which meant a recall for Fatboy, but coming off three good League performances we had every right to feel that our name was on the Cup. Yet no one could have hoped for the stunning 3-1 win in Poland, certainly not when they took an early lead. Grim memories of grim knock-outs in grim Eastern European locations in the past came back to haunt us. This was without doubt one of the grottiest arm-pits we'd been sent to visit, though the widely predicted trouble totally failed to materialise as the Poles seemed more intent on bothering the police than taking on the Reds. Sharpe and McClair immediately cast any doubts from our mind, repeating their double-act from the previous round to equalise. When their sweeper got the red card for his assault on Sharpe, the game was ours. A cracking blow from Sparky and a final piss-taking, tie-clinching third from Brucey sealed our passage to the final. The return, in the post-Wembley hangover, was a formality.

The final was to be in Rotterdam against Barcelona; Laudrup, Koeman and all. Instantly minds went back to 1984, the last great European night at Old Trafford. Once again, we'd be underdogs; once again, United would provide us with a night of unforgettable drama and glory.

* * * * *

RED-EYE

"Rotterdam memories are a sea of impressions. 30,000 Reds jamming the roads to the coast. Coaches, minibuses and charabancs plastered in red and white from every port and town. Amsterdam invaded by horny Reds filling every hole available. The sweet smell of substance abuse in every nostril.

Crates of beer being unloaded, drunk and discarded in every Rotterdam street. Bemused Barca fans treating us like brothers. Mad Dutch police singing United anthems and doing the conga. More drink, more smokes, and even more rain. Flags and colours from every corner of the Red planet. The stadium totally taken over by rampant Reds, Barca completely out-sung. Deafening choruses of "Always Look on the Bright Side" , drunken and full-throated. Amazing vibes from everyone there; stupid grins and instant friendships the order of the day. Sparky...he's taken it too far ... f*ck me, it's in! Clayton on the line, we'll love him forever. So drenched it's unbelievable but we're too drunk to care. Robson lifts the red-ribboned Cup. There's blokes around in tears. Staggering around in a haze afterwards - some locals come out and applaud us, a bloke presses bottles of Oranjeboon into our hands. Can't believe we made it home. Can't believe there'll be another night like that again, ever."

Ged, Salford

* * * * *

At the post-Rotterdam parade when those who'd been left behind came to extend the party ever onwards, there were even some City fans spotted, presumably following the Stone Roses viewpoint that the Final had been "good for Manchester" as a city. Naturally, the vast majority of our embittered neighbours failed to see our triumph in such a positive light. Most had spent the night of the 15th grumbling at their unlicensed TV sets, cheering on Koeman (what irony!) and howling in agony when the whistle went. Within hours, the Bluenose intellectuals, who are condemned to a life of dreaming up pathetic arguments to deflect attention away from their inferiority, had come up with the new Blue view. The Euro Cup Winners' Cup was a poxy trophy, the worst of the three Euro Cups and besides, Barca were rubbish and all our other opponents second-rate.

This was City at their most pitiful. For 20 years, they'd been claiming their 1970 ECWC win was the last word in glory; now, suddenly it had become a worthless Cup. And who were City's mighty opponents in 1970? The famous Gornik Zabrze. Well, famous at least in comparison to the other sides City knocked out – Schalke 04, Academica Coimbra (!) and Lierse. Who? You might well ask. The final itself was played in an empty Vienna stadium in front of 10,000; only 4,000 Bluenoses could be arsed to make the trip. Just to rub in the final's insignificance, City's win was virtually ignored since the FA Cup Replay at Old Trafford took place that night. City's moment of Euro glory *(sic)* was the only English Euro win not to be shown live on TV. Compare that to Rotterdam; let's all laugh at City, with knobs on.

Barcelona, incidentally, won the following season's European Cup with virtually the same team. Some 'rubbish'.

On the team bus that toured Manchester was a young Ukranian winger who'd been signed for only £650,000 and had made an impressive debut at Selhurst Park. Few of us yet knew how to spell Andrei Kanchelskis; we certainly didn't suspect that within three years, he was to become our key to the Double. We had been complaining, rightly, that we were too dependant on just one winger, Lee Sharpe; but by the end of '90/'91, with the quiet arrivals of Giggs and Andrei, the solution to our problem was already in our grasp.

* * * * *

In May, the financial restructuring that had been inevitable since the Knighton fiasco, finally occurred. MUFC PLC was created under the aegis of Roland Smith, the BAe boss and noted Red; Edwards remained not only Chairman of the Football Club Board but was also to be Chief Executive of the PLC. This was not exactly popular; past proponents of a flotation had envisaged a separation of powers that would dilute Edwards' position rather more than that. In the event, the only dilution was in the number of shares Edwards held but he was still left with enough to remain the pre-eminent figure at OT. What he had managed to do was reap an enormous reward of £6 million for his off-loaded shares. No doubt the prospectus

CAN YOU GUESS WHAT _TEAM_ THIS MAN SUPPORTS AND WHAT _MATCH_ HE IS WATCHING?

©DRASTIC

THE TEAMS COME ONTO THE PITCH..

AND THE TEAM'S WARM UP...

THE MATCH BEGINS...

TEN MINUTES INTO THE FIRST HALF...

"...AND THE FIRST CHANCE AFTER 11 MINUTES..

THE FIRST HALF COMES TO AN END...

..AND ITS TIME FOR THE HALF TIME INTERVAL...

THE SECOND HALF BEGINS...

AND SOON THEY ARE INTO THE FINAL 25 MINUTES OF TIME...

.. AND THEN THE FIRST GOAL!.. "...AND ONLY TWENTY-FIVE MINUTES LEFT.. GULP!

... WHEN OUT OF THE "BLUE"...

" ANOTHER GOAL! AAAGGHHH!

...THE DRAMA HADN'T FINISHED YET WITH ONLY TEN MINUTES LEFT, THERE WAS ANOTHER GOAL! CHEER! CHEER! CHEER!

TICK TICK ...TIME IS TICKING AWAY WHEN ALL OF A SUDDEN IN THE LAST MINUTE..

...THE BALL IS CLEARED OFF THE LINE!!... NOOOO!!!

AND THE FINAL WHISTLE BLOWS!...

ANSWER:
A **MANCHESTER CITY SUPPORTER** WATCHING **MANCHESTER UTD** V **BARCELONA** EUROPEAN CUP WINNERS CUP FINAL 1991

84

promise that Edwards would be getting as much of the proceeds as the Strettie redevelopment hardly encouraged the average fan to invest. The share issue seemed designed to work against the terrace Red. At a time when fans needed to find cash for Rotterdam and LMTB renewals, they were being offered the chance to invest at a price of almost £200. In the circumstances, it was amazing that 10,000 apparently were still able to become shareholders.

Within days of the flotation, the spirit behind it became much clearer. The shares had been drastically over-priced with the result that 54% of the 2.6 million shares had to be taken up by City under-writers. Instead of shares being in the hands of potentially troublesome Reds, safe, faceless bankers had them. Edwards was able to pocket millions for his shares from the under-writers thanks to this 30% over-valuation. Edwards had pulled off his greatest financial coup; he'd made a fortune and yet had managed to stay in control. Furthermore, he could continue to draw an enormous Chief Exec's salary and reap whatever dividends accrued on the 25% share-holding he still had. There could be no doubt that he was the clear flotation winner. As for us, we faced the uncertain prospect of supporting a Club that now had to be run like any City-quoted firm, under the control of a PLC. All that was certain was that transfer funds were at the mercy of the accountants and that every year would see a cash outflow from the coffers to pay dividends. The dreams of a Club owned by fans and run solely for the benefit of the team had been dashed. It will be interesting to see what the implications of this set-up are if we hit a couple of lean seasons; we might end up hankering for the days when it was only the Edwards family who controlled the purse-strings.

A final word for whoever was responsible for allowing Rod Stewart to gig at Old Trafford in the summer, thus preventing any action being taken about the atrocious state of our pitch. You cost us the '91/'92 Championship. Well done.

* * * * *

Later in the season, *Red Issue* became embroiled in yet another controversy when the 'half-decent football mag' (a semi-accurate description) *When Saturday Comes* announced sanctimoniously that it would no longer list *RI* on its back pages since it did not wish to be seen 'endorsing' our fanzine. Apparently there had been complaints about the so-called vulgarity and anti-Scouse hostility: Piccadilly Records, a source of *RI* for many bitter Blues too, soon followed suit. After an exchange of flack in the respective organs' columns, the *RI* editors sat back, cheerfully contemplating the boost in sales that this additional notoriety had engendered.

Amazingly, *WSC* was once seen as a ground-breaking pioneer, leading the way for hundreds of club fanzines to follow. Indeed, at the time of its inception, there was clearly a role to be filled of spokesman for football fandom as a whole in the battle against hostile authority: *WSC* was even, on occasion, funny. By 1991 and the *Red Ish* dispute, it had become clear just how far *WSC* had drifted from the true fanzine spirit. If we accept *Foul*, the punk fanzines and perhaps even *The End* as being the gene-bearing ancestors of the '80s zines, who now is closer in tone, humour and vigour to those forebears: *WSC* or *RI*?

The answer is obvious. Turning to *WSC* after reading *RI* is like switching from a particularly good fart-filled episode of *The Young Ones* to a Sunday repeat of *Last of the Summer Wine*. If you are truly interested in Third Division toilet facilities or Tunisian Youth tournaments, then the tepid, half-hearted pages of *WSC* are for you. These poor, Scouse-loving people in their City of London offices seem to have lost all connection to the terrace from which they allegedly sprung; the mind boggles when trying to visualise the mindset and morality of supposed footie fans who could find *RI* so offensive that they can't bear to see the very title printed in their mag.

Leaving aside the salient fact that equally 'offensive' zines remain listed – and presumably endorsed – by *WSC*, consider the absurdity of pretending that the nation's top zine doesn't exist. It's reminiscent of *Top of the Pops* trying desperately to ignore the fact that the Pistols' *God Save the Queen* was the best-selling record in Jubilee Week. In the final analysis, all this does is reflect poorly on *WSC*. By exhibiting the pomposity of Jimmy Hill and the suburban moralising of Mary White-house, they simply demonstrate what they have become – an anachronism that makes even *90 Minutes* seem daring.

There is, of course, a larger ideological spirit that underpins this sort of spat. All too often, organisations and publications that seek to represent football fans as a whole tend to disparage so-called 'sectarian' forces like *Red Ish*, accusing them of dividing fandom and thus reducing supporter power in general. The self-styled 'football academics' are particularly prone to this kind of Marxist world view: footie fans are the working-classes of the soccer world who should recognise the football establishment and its lackeys as the common enemy. Instead of directing our energies to lambasting fellow supporters from other tribes, we should be acting together as an international-ist force to overthrow our oppressors, break our chains and carry out a glorious proletarian revolution etc., etc., *ad nau-seam*. Such is the driving force behind all those bespectacled types with sociology degrees who rush around setting up poxy fan groups and spreading the gospel of inter-club love-ins and who find the United/Scouse/Scum rivalries distasteful in the extreme.

This, then, is the world of the WSC devotee – and they're welcome to it. The truth is that in football, as in world politics in general, the working classes are not suffering from 'false consciousness' and do not just need to be led into international brotherhood by the intellectual elite. What "the masses" know is that nationalism and tribalism are forces far greater than any other and that it is pointless to seek to work against the natural grain. Sure, there may be temporary alliances to halt the more brainless schemes of the senile F.A. or the cretins in Whitehall but there can be no permanent departure from the natural state of the true football fan – that his support of the club is as much shaped by his hatred of others as by his love for his own team.

After all, if there's one creature even more despicable than the fervent Mickey or Bluenose, it's the bloody 'neutral' football supporter, for whom *WSC* is the house journal. This is the person who will talk of all fans working together in harmony, who will argue that clubs should sacrifice their interests for the national team, who will demand clubs like ours cough up to subsidise the lower division wasters who play at garden sheds. For any true Red, the correct response is "bollocks to all that". Who cares if 20 clubs go into liquidation, England get beaten by Rwanda and inter-club bitterness gets so bad that any Scouser entering Manc needs an armed police escort? As long as United beat the Unholy Trinity and then win the European Cup, so what?

Elsewhere in '90/91:

◻ Kenny Dalglish walks out on Anfield, unable to take the pressure any longer – surely not anything to do with not having the bottle to rebuild a team on a budget...Graeme Sourness later becomes our favourite 'Pool manager ever.

◻ In the world of commodities trading, Lazio set a record for larded pork bellies futures by bidding £8.5 million for Gazza.

◻ Gordon Strachan is voted Footballer of the Year but other OT alumnus Norman Whiteside retires through injury, ending our dream that he might one day return to us.

◻ World Cup Cheat Diego Maradona's Hand of God is overshadowed by his nose. He tests positive for cocaine abuse and is banned for 15 months.

◻ Tony Adams is tested for drink-driving and ends up in the clink; the judge dismisses his appeal that the police were offside.

◻ Arsenal win the League, the turning point being a 3-0

hammering of Liverpool; the game is now cited as marking the end of the Anfield Era. Nice one you Gooners.

◻ Sourness spends £5 million in July on Saunders and Mark Wright. The Comedy of Errors had begun.

◻ Venables and Sugar 'save' Spurs; obviously a meaning of the 'save' that had previously escaped us.

◻ Howard Kendall walks out on City claiming he's going back to 'the wife' – Everton. City remain the slut-on-the-side whom everyone screws but no one loves.

◻ UEFA bring in the foreigners rule, a typically snotty piece of anti-British legislation designed to stop us winning all the trophies like we used to do.

◻ Eric Cantona rejoins Marseilles and is almost immediately banned from the national team for calling the manager a *sac de merde* (= 'shit-bag').

1991/92

You were tempted not to read this bit weren't you? 1992, as the Queen put it, was the ultimate *annus horribilis*. They say you have to experience the lows in life to get the most from the highs and there may be something in that. 1977 was all the sweeter for avenging the 'cup of tears', the '83 Cup Final ample compensation for the Milk Cup robbery. But those last months of the '91/'92 season served no purpose that I can see. It was slow, gruelling torture of the most unbearable kind. No Scouser could have devised it better.

In retrospect, it all seems to have been part of a general cosmic plot to make '92 the most bastard year of the century. The Tories did a Leeds and stole an election they seemed certain to lose – and subsequently played as badly as Leeds once they'd won it. The Strettie was demolished in the face of total consumer opposition – so much for democracy. And to make a miserable summer worse, England embarrassed the nation in Sweden, having left out Parker and Pally to add insult to injury. Had World War Three broken out at some point, it would have been perfectly appropriate.

In those lazy, hazy dog-days of summer '91, with the Rotterdam buzz still tickling every Red fancy, it had all seemed so promising. Fergie had made his first wholly successful transfer swoop of his OT career, adding a bargain Peter Schmeichel and Paul Parker to his earlier capture of Andrei. For the first time in living memory, we had a world-class keeper, a solid back four and THREE wingers to choose from; Ince had begun to fulfil his potential at last and Hughesy had just had one of his best years ever. Who could blame us for feeling confident? It was exactly 25 years since our last title, this was to be the final

Football League championship and it was the curtain call of the Stretford End – all the omens were propitious for a title presentation in May in front of the ultimate Strettie audience. For five months of the season, this dream appeared to be on the brink of realisation.

August alone proved the hard evidence from which our title hopes were woven. Robson's cracking drive in the opener, then his battling endurance and leadership against the Sheep that led finally to his own 85th minute equaliser exemplified the centrality of Robbo to our play; it was almost as if he knew this was his last chance to lead us to the Grail from the captain's bridge and he played every game as if his life depended on the result. He missed 20 games however – and we missed him. At Goodison, the cross-burners bombarded us mercilessly but the point was saved by Schmeichel and an increasingly sure-footed backline – any other past season, we would have lost.

Lingering doubts about Irwin apart, the team's bedrock finally seemed secure. In the first 14 games, United only conceded three goals, a ratio of almost Gunnerish parsimony. Meanwhile, Arsenal themselves and Liverpool were both off-peak – Leeds, whom we'd outplayed and outfought in the blazing heat of OT at the end of August were shaping up to be our only rivals. With Giggs roasting fullbacks and scoring the occasional classic like the acutely-angled second against Norwich, we only needed Choccy and Hughesy to sharpen up for us to capitalise fully on our midfield dominance. The title trophy gleamed alluringly.

Unfortunately, other trophies demanded our attention too, later to the detriment of our League priorities. We begun our European defence in Athens, which was beneficial only for our tans and our insomnia, although it was amusing to discover that there was indeed a pitch in the world in worse state than OT's. Three days later, Luton came for their annual reminder of their uselessness. 5-0 flattered them. Can't something be done to keep these dreadful suburbanites out of the big boys division? Mid-week, amidst scenes of chaos outside, Cambridge were dispatched 3-0 in the League Cup. Thousands were still attempting to gain entry after 20 minutes play; token-fever was the cause. Another triumph of OT organisation which at least hastened the demise of the token-in-the-programme farce.

Three days later came the eagerly-awaited trip to White Hart Lane. Incredibly, Spurs were in second place at the time thus occasioning a great deal of Cockney mouthing-off about their prospects. It was a golden afternoon, typifying the almost innocent spirit of the times before the angst and suffering of the New Year clouded our vision.

* * * * *

RED-EYE

"At 99.9% of away games I usually view the match through half-closed eyes as a result of too much ale in the hours preceding kick off. This one, however, was different. United were allocated approximately 3,000 tickets for this game which were snapped up almost instantly. Hardly surprising since United were top of the League and still on a wave of euphoria from events in Holland the previous May.

United's board once again proved themselves to be to customer care what Michael Jackson is to child-minding with the pompous statement: "All tickets have been sold and United fans without tickets are urged not to travel as there will be no cash admissions on the day of the game."

Undeterred we set off on the 7:40 InterCity to Euston in the faint hope of picking up tickets from an 'entrepreneur' outside the magnificent arena that is White Hart Lane.

Upon reaching the ground shortly before mid-day we were astounded to see turnstiles clearly marked 'cash' and huge queues – even at that time – snaking around the ground. Having no other option we had to forsake our pre-match prescription of alcohol and junk food and join the snake's tail. It was minutes after entering the ground at 12-20pm that the gates slammed shut behind us leaving hundreds of other hopeful Reds who had decided to 'chance it' locked outside.

Once inside the ground the atmosphere was a bit muted probably because there were 35,000 sober people in there patiently waiting the two or so hours before kick off.

Things livened up however when Warren Mitchell (Alf Garnett and a Spurs fan in real life) came on to the pitch and referred to the Manchester contingent as "Yobboes". The brain-dead Spurs fans, thinking he really supported West Ham, booed him while all the cheers came from the United end!

This kick-started the atmosphere and in no time the match was under way. United took an early lead through Hughes and dominated the first half. It was then that one of the strangest refereeing decisions I have ever seen was given. A Spurs player committed a foul on the half-way line and was astonishingly given a free kick. This was taken while the ball was still moving and was passed straight to Gordon Durie who was offside. The goal, amazingly, was allowed to stand.

In the second half United continued to press for the winner but despite ex-bitter blue Paul Stewart being sent off they missed a string of chances. Then, with four minutes to go, a Bryan Robson trademark glancing header silenced the Spurs fans and sent 5,000 Reds into ecstasy. (It is a standing joke among the LH Reds about the number of United fans at this game and it has been exaggerated that much that at the last count there were 62,000 Reds present).

A brilliant game, a brilliant day out and not one drop of alcohol had passed my lips. I remember similar incidents at St James's Park and Bramall Lane where I stayed off the hard stuff and loved every second.

The next United away game after Spurs was at the Abbey Stadium Cambridge. I had my usual seven or eight pints and stood through 90 minutes of crap, desperately wishing I was somewhere else. I don't think I'll ever learn."

Jamie Smith, Little Hulton

* * * * *

Strangely enough, for the next seven weeks or so, United failed to break out of the bridgehead we'd established, dropping nine points in five games and also falling on our Euroarses for good measure. Grumblings from K-stand about a return to the crap old days were audible; Hughes was not getting them in up front and Kanchelskis had to miss three matches – tellingly, our worst team performances. In the return against Athinaikos, panic was in the OT air as the Greeks-bearing-no-gifts took us to extra time before we won 2-0. Home draws against the Arse and Liverpool disappointed; if only we'd caught them at Christmas. In Madrid, trailing only 1-0 with minutes to go after Webb had hit the woodwork, we got sucker-punched twice, leaving us with an impossible task for the return. In the circumstances we did well to lift ourselves sufficiently to go 2-1 up at Hillsborough before Jemson's late double caused our first League defeat of '91 /'92.

Mark Robins made a welcome return with a brace against Portsmouth in the League Cup and we scored a tentative win against the Blades, more memorable for the opportunity an on-pitch Edwards gave us before the kick-off to express our appreciation of his work... But the next three games planted seeds, flowers and fully-grown trees of doubt in our minds. For a few moments against Athletico, an epic night of Barcelonian proportions seemed possible when Hughes put us ahead; Schuster then took charge and the night fizzled out to the flatness of a can of Red Devil. Many of us blamed the missing 8,000 part-timers but in truth we weren't in it. Red Star Belgrade ground our faces further into the mire in the Super Cup. We won but were left in no doubt as to who had the worthier pretensions to a European kingdom. In between those two lessons was sandwiched the most tedious passion-free derby match any of us could remember. All the more surprising, then, that within days, the team erupted with a burst of thrilling, wing-driven football that lit up the winter skies.

Before the kick-off against West Ham, we regaled the visitors with a song about Bluenose rejects Morley and Bishop which seemed to imply unsavoury practices of a Liverpudlian kind – what could this possibly have meant? "Any old irons" -?! Andrei was back doing his celebrated impression of a 125 and Giggs was at his impudent best, scoring with a devastating mid-air volley. The scoreline was a travesty – it had been the most annihilating 2-1 of all time. At Selhurst Park, Andrei finally scored his first of the season as the Reds magisterially won 3-1; he got another in the League Cup against Oldham. Three days later came a *tour de force* against Coventry and a thumping 4-0 victory. A fourth good game in a row from Neil Webb, now so fat that after lifting his goal into the Strettie net and leaping into Pally's arms, the big man could scarcely hold him off the ground. A supremely cheeky diving header in front of the paddock – by now usually filled with Reds – marked Hughesy's first in the League since the Spurs game. United were scoring at last.

At Stamford Bridge, we took full revenge for the Blues double over us in '90/'91. Denis finally showed us what he could do with a free-kick and silenced the last of his critics, Hughesy's inspired back-heel set up Choccy and United spared Chelsea by settling for 3-1. The main course was saved for Boxing Day in a throwback to those ridiculous '60s festive double-headers when United would lose 6-1 and win 5-1 against the same team on consecutive days (this actually happened once). Boundary Park witnessed the '91/'92 side at its joyous, carefree, zest-filled best. We won 6-3, it could have been 10-5, and three of our goals were pure gold.

Andrei danced and dazzled his way through a bemused Latics defence to score a solo spectacular, a prototype of his magical Maine Road '94 classic. Denis netted a free-kick of even better quality than his Chelsea-buster and Ryan Giggs, in front of the Red end, theatrically and precisely rounded the keeper for number six. Leeds, about to face us in the first of the epic trilogy of confrontations, must have feared the worst. With hindsight, we now know that we'd peaked far too soon – the three Leeds games were treated as though they were the climax of the season when, in fact, they could only be part of the foreplay.

The tension engendered by the massively hyped anticipation leading up to the three games was unbelievable. THREE visits to Elland Road in 17 days; now you could appreciate how Hercules felt when the gods told him he had a few odd jobs to do. No one needed reminding of the welcome the bestial Yorkie yobs had given us back in February or of the complacent laxity of the local constabulary. Moreover, this time the Leeds team were a far more formidable proposition, unbeaten in months and in no doubt as to the importance their sheep-worrying support placed upon beating us. Only the most madly fervent Reds could have expected that we would return from these expeditions virtually unbloodied and certainly defiantly unbowed. We had been tested to destruction and not found wanting; we had proved beyond all doubt to ourselves, to Leeds and to the watching millions that we were the best team in Britain. The ultimate, unexpected destination of the title did not change that fundamental truth and the subsequent seasons, as we know, offered further proof to any remaining naysayers.

In Round One, the League tie, Fatboy's volley put us ahead and somehow we failed to finish them off. They were only in the game for 20 minutes and had to rely on a penalty to salvage some scraps of pride. A moral victory for the Reds.

In Round Two, the League Cup quarter-final, Clayton was instantly forgiven for his QPR blunders by blasting a free-kick equaliser. United wrapped their tentacles around the game, squeezing the life from an increasingly desperate Sheep side; Giggs in particular, revelled in the limelight, setting up Andrie's goal. We won 3-1 – Sgt. Wilko conceded our utter superiority.

In Round Three, the FA Cup tie of the season, Leeds were perhaps the better side but could not break through. Hughesy headed home Giggs' cross for the only goal of the game. The scum's bitterness knew no bounds – the Elland Road horde had not seen United beaten for 12 years and they'd blown three chances to rectify things in a fortnight. A slightly more efficient police presence prevented them physically expressing their rage; our joy was complete, our supremacy sealed.

* * * * *

In between the first and second Leeds games, United had welcomed in the New Year with the visit of QPR. In front of a hung-over TV audience expecting a goalfest, five were duly scored. Unfortunately, four of them were by the Londoners. Shell-shocked would be too soft an adjective to describe our state of mind as we filed out. Why had Andrei and Giggs been left out of the starting line-up – was Alex now back in his Tinkerbell mode? What on earth had Clayton been doing on New Year's Eve to play so atrociously even by his standards? – had he been up to a touch of the George Best's down at the Royale? In fact, what were the entire team on? Had they all been out on a tour of Sharpey's favourite haunts? Rumours were soon rife that a combination of Alex's birthday bash and usual Hogmanay festivities had led to some over-indulgence at the Midland, naturally all vociferously denied by the Club who cited a flu outbreak as the cause. In itself, the game could hardly be said to be the harbinger of the forthcoming catastrophe – after all, the two Leeds wins came *after* QPR – but United, with only a couple of exceptions, never played a confident League game again. On that dark January afternoon, the storm clouds were gathering already.

Up until this point, the support had been magnificent, even at home. The travelling Reds had swelled to enormous proportions and at Notts County, there was chaos as over 3,000 Reds were locked out. An annihilation of the moribund Magpies was arrogantly demanded but never materialised, Clayton's lateish penalty being required to save a point. It felt like the doom-laden moment of the season, the first time that both team and fans looked and acted as if anxiety and doubt were beginning to take a grip of our spirits. Not that this was overwhelming yet; in fact, what made it worse was that it was all so gradual, a slow and deliberate increase in tension, worry and discontent that seeped into OT throughout February and March. For now, there was no crisis as Hughesy's goal beat Villa and worthy draws were secured at The Dell and Highbury. But as United went into a four-game home run in February, the team's play and our own composure were clearly deteriorating.

The Saints came to OT for the FA Cup replay and proceeded to outplay us to take a two goal lead; even at 2-1, despair filled the air. But when Choccy forced home the injury-time equaliser at the Strettie end, utter terrace bedlam ensued. For at least three minutes our heads were somewhere in the stratosphere – the ecstatic relief was akin to what we felt in the Oldham semi in '94. We were out of jail, psychologically boosted to a state of nirvana.

We dominated extra-time, Robbo scored...and David Elleray (!) disallowed it for not crossing the line. Photographs later proved that the ball was virtually in the Strettie end and down the tunnel, let alone in the net. To our horror, we lost the ensuing penalty shoot-out 4-2, forced to endure Shearer's arrestable gesture to us and Giggsy's miss. Later, Fergie cheerfully admitted that United made few contingency plans for shoot-outs and apparently this policy of criminal neglect was to continue, if Torpedo was anything to go by. Objectively, it may well have been 'a good thing' to go out of the Cup and concentrate on the League but against Wednesday four days later, it seemed clear that the KO had done nothing for the team's confidence, or for ours.

We were now in the full throes of an anxiety attack; the support against the Owls and Chelsea three weeks later was poor. Robbo, shamefully, was actually booed and later had the humiliating task of appealing for our uncritical support publicly. We did at least beat Palace but required a last-ditch Hughesy effort to escape against Chelsea. That was Sparky's last hurrah as he spent much of the rest of his season lost in the fog of war, pursuing on-pitch vendettas or stuck on his arse, seemingly torn up inside by his inability to rescue the title for us. Andrei was beginning to run himself into the ground, increasingly a desolate figure. As a collective, the team looked tired, worried and pressurised; the earlier sweetly measured football began to be replaced by impatient, premature upfield punting from players whose imaginations were failing them. Going into March, Andrei actually asked to be left out, desperately requiring time to refuel and rejuvenate. Our title odds lengthened just a touch.

Then, for a few March days, the clouds lifted. Lee Sharpe came back to his best; the prospect of Wembley lifted the spirits and the Red support found renewed voice. At Sheffield United, we gave our most commanding performance for months, keeping our heads to overturn the Blades' lead, roared on by the Red and White Army who had enjoyed one of their finest moments three days earlier.

* * * * *

RED-EYE

"We'd drawn 0-0 in the first leg of the Rumbelows Semi at Boro so now we were in for a cracker at OT. But nothing could have prepared me for such an amazing night.

In the first half, I was getting rather pissed off with The Boro outsinging us. They had K Stand and the Scoreboard End. They equalised in the second half and we were approaching extra time when a group of about 10 Reds in front of me started jumping up and down singing 'Ferguson's Red and White Army'. No one joined in at first but they carried on regardless.

Extra time arrived and this group was growing by the minute now. The game was struggling, the pitch was shit, the players were knackered but these lads kept singing and bouncing non-stop; it was getting louder and louder and then the whole stadium seemed to erupt. Lads were singing and dancing in the aisles everywhere; G and H, the Main Stand, the Paddock, they were all singing it — you couldn't hear yourself think. Most of us were sweating like a bollock by now but we didn't care. The Boro fans just stood in disbelief, silent.

There was this old bloke not far away from me waving his crutches in the air, bouncing up and down on one leg, singing his heart out. And then to top it off, Giggs scored at the Stretford End — it was party time. 'Que Sera Sera' burst out; a huge red and white ribbon was hoisted up by the Stretty Barmy

Army. 'We're the famous Stretford End!' was sung at the top of our voices. We were going to Wembley.

That was the last great Stretford End night. The last game against Spurs was the final curtain for the End. It was a sad day for many a Red but we tried to have a good laugh singing chants from the '70s and '80s – as well as 'You can stick your fucking seats up yer arse' aimed at Edwards. After the final whistle, we sang on till the police moved us. One bloke was on all fours kissing the ground. A policeman tried to move him but he was in tears, saying "You don't understand what this means for us. I've stood here for years." We all had lumps in our throats. As we left the ground, I tied my scarf to the railings and a flag I'd made which simply said: 'We're the famous Stretford End"

'Loony' Jason Davies, Northwich

* * * * *

The same night as our Rumbelows triumph, the Sheep had been hammered 4-1. We now had the opportunity to cut loose. In the next three games, we failed to score and took only two points; Robson got injured and the pitch reached a new level of unplayable disgrace. In the midst of this nightmare, Neil Webb lost whatever remaining support he had by going to Graham Taylor behind Fergie's back to proclaim his availability for the Czech game, this after Alex had rightly withdrawn everyone at OT from international duty.

The 3-1 win at Norwich on the 31st settled every fevered brow. Incey scored twice, we looked like a team again and Leeds lost heavily to the Bitters four days later. Firmly in pole position with points, games and goals in hand, surely we would be safe.

A feverish, scorching, temperamental derby match was drawn 1-1, Pointon's sending off serving only to galvanise a previously outplayed Bluenose team who levelled after Brucey gave away a cretinous penalty. Two lost points but still no need to panic yet. The summit was in sight – six games in 14 days lay in between. Victims of our own success and of the FA's crass stupidity in scheduling an England match on the 29th, we still felt we could do it as long as we remained injury-free; it was still ours to lose not Leeds' to win. Typically, our only truly champion performance of that fateful fortnight was at Wembley. In a game for the connoisseur rather than the passionate, we beat Forest 1-0 to right the failure of '91. Mickey Phelan played the game of his life – it was a surreal day alright. There was something vaguely indecent about taking a Wembley day-off in the eye of such a League fixture storm. We won a trophy, we had a trip to The Twin Towers, but frankly, we'd have done better to have had the weekend free for a League match. The League Cup was surely the most low-key trophy win in memory; we'd all have swapped it for a couple of extra points.

And so into a Dantean inferno of disaster. Black days of grief that passed as a blur of misery, much of it spent with head in hands feeling sick to the pit of the stomach. The only win came against the Saints, Andrei scoring to be lauded as a 'true match-winner' by Fergie, making his decision to leave him out against Luton and West Ham all the more infuriating. Luton, an abysmal team who we'd stuffed six months before, cost us two points in the direst of games. Paul Parker was injured, adding to a casualty list that Ince had joined thanks to the clogging carthorses of Southampton. Victory over Forest on Monday became absolutely essential.

At this crucial, life-threatening juncture, Fergie chose to drop Mark Hughes. Nobody would claim he was having a good time of it but surely at moments like that Easter Monday, Sparky was the one man you would want out there. The Strettie was at its most rabidly frantic all afternoon, virtually sucking the ball into the net as McClair scored. We created a score of chances but lost – Forest, claiming a meaningless revenge for Wembley, made three openings and scored from two. After we had bayed for him for 80 minutes, Hughesy was finally allowed on, Webb petulantly sauntering off into disgrace and opprobrium. It was too late, though, for Sparky to save it. Two days later, in a bear-pit at Upton Park, we lost to the most ridiculous goal of the season as the Hammers, already relegated, lifted their game to what Alex called an 'obscene' level. We looked what we were – totally exhausted, bereft of inspiration, playing what was a game too far. Leeds were now, for the first time in the season, in the driving seat. There was no time for any pressure to build on them, no question of 'bottle' to be answered; they could merely treat their Bramhall Lane game as a Cup Final then sit back. They won 3-2 before we'd stepped on to the Anfield pitch.

Funnily enough, many felt prouder of the team that day on Merseydive than for many months past. Robson and Ince, risking their futures, had dragged themselves out of the treatment rooms, ready to offer whatever last drops of blood they had for United. We lost 2-0, having hit the woodwork three times – how typical of this wretched season. Somehow a team devastated by disappointment, with next to nothing left in the fuel tank, had still conspired to put together a battling display for the doomed Red Army. As the Kop gleefully sang 'You lost the League on Merseyside' and revelled in the irony of their singing 'Always look on the bright side', our only consolation amidst the desolation was the knowledge that nothing could be as bad as this again.

That season we'd won the League Cup, the Super Cup, the Youth Cup and both PFA Awards for Pally and Giggs; we'd seen the two most exciting wingers of our generation emerge and shine; we'd won the Trans-Pennine Trilogy and had witnessed some devastating attacking team displays. But at that moment in April, all that achievement was dwarfed by the hideous truth that we'd lost the title to Leeds because of a defeat at Liverpool. There was no worse conjunction of misfortune possible. It was simply the worst Red moment for 18 years. There was nothing you could say to the jubilant Bitters, Scum and Dirties; there could only be one answer possible – the title HAD to be won in '93. What had always been an obsessive desire was now an absolute necessity. In the meantime, the Red three-quarters of Manchester endured the most woeful summer of our time. Revenge was to be a dish served best cold.

Elsewhere in 1991/92

▢ Blackburn Rovers, despite losing 14 Second Division games, slime their way into the top flight via the play-offs under Kenny Dalglish. Their average gate the previous season had been 8,500, making Ewood Park now the part-timers' capital of the nation.

▢ 400 Brummies riot at St Andrews against Stoke; the referee is attacked making this the first constructive pitch invasion ever.

▢ Graeme Sourness has heart surgery. Thankfully he survives the stress of the FA Cup run to continue his excellent work at Anfield. He also manages to offend the Hillsborough shrine tenders by giving an interview to *The Sun* about his marriage break-up. Tasteful.

▢ The Premier League is founded and the Sky deal announced. Radical innovations such as five minutes more half-time and refs in green change the face of football forever..ha. United are thus condemned to years of Murdoch screwing up our fixture list, awaydays to The Dell on a Monday night etc., etc.

▢ The mighty City, such a big club of course, get knocked out of both Cups by lower division Middlesborough. The Maine Road moths in the trophy cupboard live on.

▢ England, with the help of such luminaries as Keith Curle and Martin Keown, are humiliated in Sweden, thus serving Turniphead right for only picking Webb from OT. Peter Schmeichel leads the Danes to glory.

▢ Leeds, Champions, unbeaten at home and the only football club in the city, pull an average gate of 29,000 – 15,000 less than United and even less than Sheff. Wed. Pathetic.

▢ Cantona-fever sweeps Yorkshire. T-shirts flood off the presses, songs are written, records planned, special Eric merchandise fills the catalogues...tee-hee.

'Man City plan to
get hooked up to
Metrolink system
and introduce a
park & ride scheme'
(M.E.N.Feb 94)

The Maine Road
Metrolink Spur -
suggested plan:

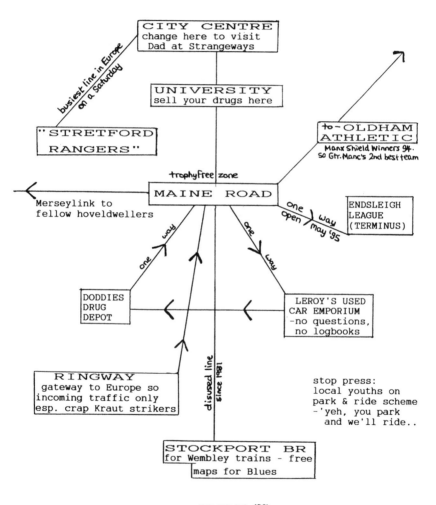

CITY CENTRE
change here to visit
Dad at Strangeways

busiest line in Europe
on a Saturday

UNIVERSITY
sell your drugs here

"STRETFORD
RANGERS"

to-OLDHAM
ATHLETIC
Manx Shield Winners 94.
So Gtr.Manc's 2nd best team

trophyfree zone

MAINE ROAD

Merseylink to
fellow hoveldwellers

one
open / way
may '95

ENDSLEIGH
LEAGUE
(TERMINUS)

one
way

one
way

DODDIES
DRUG
DEPOT

LEROY'S USED
CAR EMPORIUM
-no questions,
no logbooks

RINGWAY
gateway to Europe so
incoming traffic only
esp. crap Kraut strikers

disused line
since 1981

stop press:
local youths on
park & ride scheme
-'yeh, you park
   and we'll ride..

STOCKPORT BR
for Wembley trains - free
maps for Blues

©RED-EYE July 1994

104

1992/93

In the ancient Greek Myth of Sisyphus, a bloke is condemned to an eternity of trying to push a mammoth boulder up a steep hill; every time he gets near the summit, he is overwhelmed by fatigue, the boulder crashes down to the bottom and he has to start all over again. I forget what philosophical point there is to this; I just knew how the bloke must have felt, for the entire legend seems to be a perfect metaphor of United's position every summer. Come August 1992, we were back at the starting line once more, on zero points, preparing for yet another painful clamber up the Championship Mountain – all that effort, all those points we had won in '91/'92 now counted for nothing. Just how long did the gods intend to keep punishing us? Wasn't a quarter of a century long enough?

Our tempers had not been improved by the various summer shenanigans at OT. Unsurprisingly, the last-ditch appeals for the salvation of the Strettie had gone unheeded. Most of us were convinced that had United added their voice to the demands of Palace and City that some terracing be preserved, we could have stemmed the all-seater tide but, of course, there was little indication that anyone in the boardroom was at all interested. The shock of seeing the hole left by the End was immense; it felt as if the ground had been halved in size, atmosphere and sheer presence. We would be kicking off with a capacity of 34,000 but the figures hid the true extent of the demolition; for three months at least, OT would be a ground without a heart. Whatever waves of vocal power we created would be lost in the Salford winds billowing through the barren west-end wound.

The Board, never slow to finesse a fiscal trick, took the

opportunity to plead reduced capacity as an excuse to jack up admission prices by up to 50%. Was this some sadist's idea of a reward for our unbending loyalty throughout the most heart-breaking season ever? As if destroying the Strettie was not enough aggravation to be going on with! As an extra touch of financial insurance, a total of three new kits were to be introduced in 1992/93, a piece of fashionable piss-taking of which Vivienne Westwood would have been proud and which rightly elicited howls of derision from everyone else ('Man U unveil 7th kit for League Cup replays...' etc.).

Those decisions served only to highlight the Board's complete lack of PR skill, a product of their continued failure to listen to the fans. There is a decent argument to be made that such price increases are justifiable in the long-term overview, given that demand far outstrips supply for United tickets and that the prices less successful clubs charge are comparable. But why not sugar the pill by granting regular attenders significant discounts, subsidised by a premium on the day-trippers' tickets? Add a fiver to the price for those making their annual shopping'n'facepainting day out to the Theatre of Dreams whilst knocking 10-15% off the price of LMTBs for the faithful. Any business knows that you have to take the best care of your hard-core consumers; you don't fleece them, you reward their loyalty.

Similarly with the kits; every season-ticket and LMTB holder should have been offered the opportunity to buy one at cost as a benefit for the ever-present Red. The rest of the kits sold in Britain to those who never attend can be priced as exploitatively as the Club likes; in fact, United shirts sold to the general bandwaggon-jumping public should be at least a tenner more than the rest. We couldn't care less if some Basingstoke father has to shell out to kit up his 12-year-old; more money for the Club to pay Eric's bonuses is always welcome.

We all accept that merchandising is a tacky but necessary part of a modern club and that United are market-leaders in this field. What isn't acceptable is that the die-hard match-goers are treated on the same level as the outsiders, i.e. as ripe for exploitation. Nor do we want, judging from the crowd's reaction at the Coventry match, such crass commercialisation as f*cking Fred the Red shoved down our throats *inside* the stadium. Keep the turf sacred – save the supermarket tactics and crappy catalogues for the armchair credit-card shoppers and Souvenir Shop groupies.

These gripes, that were further grit under the lids of eyes still red raw from the tears of April, were further exacerbated by the Shearer Saga. The Saints striker, clearly the hottest goal-scoring prospect of the decade, was on the move at last. United needed a 20-goal-a-year man desperately and were massively in the black. *Ergo*, Shearer would be moving to United, right? Wrong. The truth of what happened has not yet been fully revealed yet, according to Shearer himself, who spent the last few weeks of last season showering praise on United and promising to come clean one day. Interesting...

What we got at the time was a series of excuses for his eventual arrival at Ewood. Firstly, the PLC would not release funds before July 31st due to some technical accounting point that hardly endeared the concept of the PLC to the fans. Then it was said that the extra £300,000 being demanded was beyond the Club's reach – this after the Board had trousered half a million from Sky TV. Finally, Shearer was slung into the dock – he had allegedly been asking for a deal that would bust apart the Club's wage structure and therefore clearly he was just too mercenary a man to be a United player. The song 'There's Only One Greedy Bastard' had its genesis in that 'revelation'.

Frankly, the entire episode stank of equivocation and deliberate muddying of the waters. Could Shearer really have been asking for much more than Cantona now gets? If the Club were afraid of setting a wage precedent, was it beyond them to ensure that the details of any settlement remained private? When Shearer tells all, no doubt the questions will be answered; it is a sign of how much the non-signing of Shearer might continue to cost us that the issue is still such a contentious one. Nevertheless, his non-arrival meant that Hughes stayed to prove the doubters wrong; it also led to the signing of Eric. Would you swap those two for Shearer? Of course not. But that wasn't the point.

Even the positive innovations that the Board introduced brought only the most grudging of credit. Tokens would henceforth appear on the match-ticket, partially reducing the corruption of past years when programmes were being sold off in batches of 20 at crucial games. Furthermore, the Reserves would no longer play home games at Old Trafford, thus allowing the pitch to survive a full season without turning into a collection of weedy sand dunes. Fans had been clamouring for these for the best part of a decade; this final admission that we'd been right only made you despair that the authorities had been so blind to the bleedin' obvious for so long. It hardly engendered confidence in their future ability to listen to us and do the right thing did it? The Board reminded one of the Nixon White House; in the midst of the incompetence of Watergate, an insider explained the Presidency's cock-ups by simply saying "You know, the thing is, these powerful guys – they're just not that bright..."

Kick-off at Bramhall Lane approached, the team needed a class midfielder and a striker; we got Dion Dublin for a million. Be still my beating heart. For anyone who'd seen his team Cambridge play, they could be forgiven for wondering whether United's basketball team was being reassembled. As 'compensation' for Shearer this seemed like replacing Platini with Phelan. Eventually, Dion's life at OT was to develop rather strangely and he's ended up on the Cult Bench with Sealey and Clayton. At the time, though we wished him well, he hardly seemed to be the answer to our needs or prayers. It was always going to be a wretched summer after April '92 and nothing had happened during it to make us feel much better. We stepped once more on to the Sisyphian trail with some foreboding.

* * * * *

Alcohol is a remarkably versatile drug. Perfect for celebration but equally useful when you need to stew in self-pity and despondency. For the first week of the season, it appeared that United had taken the concept of drinking away the sorrow rather too far. The defence looked hung-over, awoken prematurely from beer-sodden slumber; Fergie was behaving like the proverbial bear-with-post-bevvie sore head, growling at every press inquisitor and lashing out at imaginary demons like some alky tramp.

At Bramhall Lane, Pally appeared to be under the impression he was still in pyjamas, giving away a dozy penalty and almost scoring a lazy own goal. Brian Hill, the last bastard-in-the-black (or, indeed, green) that you would want to have for your first game, refused an obvious penalty for a trip on Giggs. Alex raged uncontrollably afterwards, threatening official complaints, barring from United games, assassination of his family etc., etc. Against Everton, United's limp-dick penetration was ruthlessly punished by three goals from four breakaways, the last after Schmeichel's impression of Rene Higuita had spectacularly backfired. Quasimodo filled TV screens proclaiming the new era at Goodison whilst Fergie flitted about in the background, chasing Piccadilly Radio personnel with his killer cup and saucer sets. The Doc had criticised Pally, the Doc worked for Picc, therefore their correspondent was banned from interviews for the next match. The ambience was hardly ideal and not aided by the first League table print-out – United rock bottom with six points lost already.

Against the tractor-fanciers from Ipswich, we were just as bad. Fifty-five minutes without creating a chance at Old Trafford was the stuff of nightmares. Perhaps they'd been as affected as we were by our first full daylit view of the rubble at the Stretford End whose baleful stare seemed to infect the entire stadium. Imagine coming home to find some bastard has driven a bulldozer through your frontroom wall. For all those for whom OT is a permanent second home throughout life, that's not too fanciful a comparison. Denis saved a point with a 20-yard Mr Benn Special; Neil Webb came on but only to prove his OT career was almost over.

Eight points lost was excuse enough for the press baboons to babble excitedly about a 'new Old Trafford crisis.' The trip to The Dell, rearranged for a Monday night by Sky thus making the voyage even more difficult for us, took on the status of a make-or-break match. On a quagmire of a pitch, drenched to the skin in our natty new shirts, a match that shrieked nil-nil was won by Dion's six yard tap-in during a frantic last minute, right in front of a corner clutch of rabid Reds. Victory at last; the creeping neurosis of the first days was instantly dispelled. Now we could begin to climb.

The mythology of this special season tends to have it that United became a Champion team mid-winter with the arrival of Eric; the months BC were merely treading water, awaiting the Messiah. Whilst that may be true, it shouldn't be forgotten that the win at The Dell set off a crucial little run, every bit as important in the final analysis as the wondrous late season performances. Five wins, a maximum 15 points and not a goal conceded – without this spell, no amount of Cantona-inspired brilliance could have rescued the title later on.

Admittedly, only the Leeds game was truly memorable in terms of our football and other wins did not wholly allay our doubts about United's attacking capabilities. But what they did achieve was to restore confidence, put us back in the title race and, above all, answer any questions about our defence. Pally had woken up at last and was Man of the Match at the City Ground – as a unit, they were back to their stingy best of 12 months ago. Hughes got a last minute winner in front of a hyper-ventilating Paddock to beat Palace after a dirge of a game was darkened further by the Dublin injury. McClair, having made the worst start to the season imaginable, finally rose to the challenge at Goodison, finishing a splendid move in a 2-0 win. Best of all, United recovered from a 'flu outbreak to produce the goods against the sheep-molesters.

Uncharacteristically, Leeds gave a good awayday account of

themselves in a season which proved their unworthiness as Champions – they failed to win away and finished 17th, the worst Champ defence since City in '69 – but Ince and Ferguson Junior took control. Two goals in a thrillsome, end-to-end first half was enough to do them and wreak revenge; there was a flash of genius from an unhappy-looking Eric but the plaudits were Andrei's for his sky-hanging header. Pleasingly, Leeds never looked impressive again after that defeat, joining City and Liverpool in the also-rans losers' section for the rest of the season. But this was to be the last hurrah for the BC United.

* * * * *

One feature of the new Old Trafford whose appeal rapidly palled was the freshly-installed, state-of-the-art PA system, allegedly costing £300,000 and entrusted to Manchester's own Mike Smash, DJ Keith Fane. For about five seconds, you could think that this was actually quite a smart set-up; used with subtlety, it could have become quite an asset. Instead, out of the speakers came a dire diet of the most inane beige-rock bollocks imaginable, interspersed with tedious announcements and that bane of AM radio, the dreaded requests from assorted 10-year-olds. Endless old toss like Paul Young and Tina Turner would be bad enough but it soon became obvious that pre-match 'entertainment' was to be used as a weapon to sanitise the atmosphere.

At the first sign of a bit of tasty banter between opposing fans, up went the volume knob to 11, drowning out our chanting and destroying the proper ambience of a football occasion. The days of mass singing from 1.30 to kick off may have long gone but now even 20 minutes of build up was out of the question; the visit of Leeds was perhaps the first time that this new tactic was properly deployed, to the aggravation of every vocal Red. It's easy to imagine what a top tune-spinner could do, if he was in tune with the crowd and prepared to ride with the flow to help create a fever pitch atmosphere; instead we get a leaden weight of deafening but boring family-value muzak crushing whatever we do.

It all makes sense when taken in conjunction with the rest of the OT experience; the extortionate, piss-weak 'safe-drinking' beer, the whinging stewards determined to pin you to your seat, the daytrippers munching and farting their way through the match but never singing, the way the ex-Strettie Enders were broken up and scattered across the stadium...Old Trafford is being Americanised, swabbed with the antiseptic of family values, de-proletarianised, stuffed with the slick, plastic fast food of the stadium rock gig and generally turned into another gleaming soul-less adjunct of theme-park Britain. We are cheer-led by the PA, coralled to sit-down, stop swearing and keep off the pitch by the ranks of police, stewards and security rent-a-mongs and, more often than not, stranded in the middle of a row of non-singing aliens. You can see us in the lulls during games, dotted around the lower parts of the stadium, little clutches of three or four frantically attempting to get things going, surrounded by indifference; we can see the like-minded souls across the aisles but can never get together and reform the collective bonds of the past – we have to wait for awaydays for that.

Do the Club care that this mania for wholesomeness, this demand that nothing must occur in the stadium that would offend a six-year-old or his mother, is throttling the life out of OT? Perhaps the new East Stand Lower will be a partial remedy, allowing the troops of the Red Army to recongregate; they might even wake up K-Stand which went into retirement during this season – although this didn't stop them complaining in *Red Ish* about the poverty of the West Stand vocal strength. Whatever happens, there is a struggle going on for the soul of Old Trafford – the day-tripper versus the die-hard, the singer versus the silent and, perhaps, the neat prim family versus the group of mates. It's obvious whose side the Club is on; nevertheless, that doesn't mean we should just give up and hand the ground over to Trappist tendency. In the meantime, let us hope the Club do not take this Yankeefying any further.

No doubt some bright spark executive has already calculated how to increase revenue by, say, having food and drink sellers constantly patrolling the aisles baseball-style. 'Fans' could then refuel continually without leaving their seat – Old Trafford would become the Board's dream, a docile, silent mass of chomping, guzzling, thermos-toting, couch potatoes too laden with superstore goodies and grub to stand, mouths too full of warmed-over BSE-burgers to sing a word of an obscene chant. Play Bon Jovi on a loop, replace Fred the Red with Ronald and rename it all Old McTrafford. You can stop this by standing up, shouting 'f*ck' a lot and singing your hearts out for the lads forever!

* * * * *

Over the next few weeks, the loudest sound you could hear at a debilitated OT was that of the chickens coming home to roost. With Dublin crocked and Robins gone – to Norwich, where he scored 15 in 30 games, natch – Hughes and McClair proved to be unable to fill the goalscoring deficit. In midfield, Fergie Junior began to lose the plot and Fergie Senior reprised his Tinkerbell selection policies from the spring. It was a sign of our desperation that we began to clamour for the return of Webb, whom we'd have happily strung up four months previously. The initial prognosis of the connoisseurs in August looked as correct as ever – we needed a class midfielder and a goalscorer. We were not exactly in a decapitated-poultry situation yet for we remained unbeaten for another nine games – but in only winning one of those, it was clear something would have to give.

The Euro tie with Torpedo brought only torpor and a touch of tragedy. Two goal-less draws, the first at a soul-less OT, the second at least enlivened by the cheap vodka and cut-price oral sex specialists on offer in Moscow, produced the dreaded shoot-out. Unbelievably, United still refused to practise for these eventualities; Fergie opined that it was just a matter of bottle. Reds who'd managed to congregate together at half-time watched in horror as a 2-0 lead was tossed aside. Choccy, predictably, missed; one look at poor Pally's face made his final-curtain backpass to the Torpedo goalie inevitable. Hughesy had long since departed the field of battle, sent off by a pathetic Danish ref. Not for the first time in history, would-be conquerors of Europe had been forced into a long, sad retreat from Moscow.

Brighton, playing in what appeared to be a full-length Tesco bags, were unconvincingly beaten over two legs, although we did witness a genuine miracle in Danny Wallace's outstanding goal, the miracle being the words 'Wallace' and 'outstanding' appearing in the same sentence. Hughesy enlivened a gloomy night for the 24,000 who bothered to show up for the return with a trademark volley but by then our faltering League form was of far more concern. At Spurs, Giggsy's Bestian strike gave every commentator a spontaneous ejaculation, ruining many a sheepskin jacket; despite travelling Reds' constant barrage of vocal support throughout half-time, it all went flat, Schmeichel flapping, Spurs scoring. Still, surely a record was set that day for the most renditions of "Running Down the Wing" in an afternoon.

At Ayresome Park, Red tempers already frayed by the amount of season-ticket allocation ending up in touts' hands – there's nothing worse than a Red exploiting Red in that way – were further serrated by a hatful of misses, Hughesy's substitution and two more lost points; the reappearance of Robbo and the bottle shown by Bruce in taking his first post-Moscow penalty were scant consolation. The sight of Giggs, floating, ski-ing and skimming across a waterlogged pitch was something to behold though.

Sparky, almost sold to Marseilles in the summer and *Red Issue*'s 'Second Worst Player' of '91/'92, was by now beginning to test the patience even of his hard-core support; possibly only the ever worse form of McClair was a greater talking point. The fans had long since assumed some striker would be coming, whether it be Hirst, Deane or A.N. Other – the only question was which of the Choccy-Sparky pair would have to go? Both could play in midfield, both could still fetch big fees from elsewhere and both had their vociferous fan clubs in the stadium who regularly traded insults in the pages of the fanzines. Hughes had made a start to his redemption against Brighton; against Liverpool, he jumped straight back into the pantheon of heroes.

Once again, we'd copped a Liverpool fixture at the worst possible time. The slum-dwellers were still crowing about April and had earlier nauseated us all with their disgusting arse-kissing of the scum at the Charity Shield. Several felt cocky enough to attempt an invasion of K and J Stands, whereupon their lack of etiquette was promptly pointed out to them by helpful Reds. As United fans were turfed out in knots throughout the afternoon, a hellish performance unfolded on the pitch. Two down with 10 to go, hundreds of thermos-toters shuffled off from G and H, leaving us to pray for deliverance.

Six hundred seconds of heavenly joy were duly despatched to us. Hughes, revelling in his favourite role of saviour of lost causes, lofted home a perfect lob over Gobbleshite, who had clearly learned nothing from the '90 Rumbelows tie: when Sparky's around, don't go fannying about your area like a clown. Molby was then carted off on a stretcher to everyone's delight and the media's distaste; full marks to the OT stretcher-bearers for their weight-lifting prowess. With a minute to go, Giggsy demonstrated that he'd finally learned how to cross a ball and, of course, it was Hughesy who flung himself forward to head it into the net. So what if we'd played like Maine Roaders? We'd sent the doleful doleites home devastatingly disappointed, which was joy enough.

Naturally, this being Man United, such a reprieve was not to mark a return to form on the back of such a psychological boost but instead heralded a full-blown, run-around-screaming, bid-for-everything crisis. In the next four games, United lost three, failed to score at all, went out of the League Cup and, against Wimbledon, produced the worst performance of the year amidst the most comotose OT crowd ever witnessed. Aston Villa, shaping up as real title contenders, beat us twice. We could only claim to have played well once, in the first Villa game; we missed chances from every conceivable angle and position in all of them.

Hughes' open goal miss in the last minute of the Villa tie just after McGrath had headed against his own post seemed to encapsulate everything that was going wrong. The demand for the immediate purchase of a goalscorer became irresistible, Fergie announcing mid-crisis in a panic-stricken tone that he would be searching "high and low for a striker". This was, of course, what he should have been doing from the moment Dublin was injured. How he must have wished at that moment that he'd kept hold of Mark Robins, currently directing Norwich towards the top of the table.

With perfect timing, bang in the middle of this series of catastrophes came both the United AGM and the publication of Fergie's book. The latter, a decent effort that showed fairness and self-awareness, nevertheless provided plenty of ammunition for those seeking to resurrect a Fergie Out campaign. It was also to aggravate the wives of McGrath and Webb, which we appreciated. The scratty-haired shrill Shelley Webb, whose mercifully brief appearances on 'Standing Room Only' caused teeth-grinding everywhere, hardly helped her husband's cause by quibbling about the book on air. As for McGrath's wife, one wonders if she still feels as loyal to Paul's cause now, given what happened to their marriage. Perhaps Alex would feel justified in saying "I told you so"?

At the AGM, some adept stage-management and evasive speechifying from the Board managed to deflect some of the impact of the hostility many present clearly felt. What they could not deflect were the facts: a £45,000 pay rise for Edwards, the abolition of the blue kit after one paltry season, a massive share dividend to further swell the coffers of the rich and a resumption of the war on street-traders. This, combined with some less-than-convincing waffle about the Shearer fiasco and future ticket prices, hardly filled Red hearts with gratitude for the suits.

As the Oldham game hove into view, the team knew that a new forward would definitely be arriving as Fergie's fax machine went into bidding overdrive – the only unknown was who the man would actually be. Tellingly, McClair and Hughes reacted like horses with wads of tobacco shoved up the bum, scoring three between them in 16 minutes. Perhaps it would be unfair to say they hadn't been giving 100% up till then but let us assume they'd both found an extra 10% from somewhere. We were on the cusp of a transformation, the turning point of the modern era: November 26th 1992.

*　*　*　*　*

Now we know precisely at what moment Fate changed course and sent us forward to claim the title. Leeds had phoned Martin Edwards to enquire about Denis Irwin, amusing in itself since the Sheep had had him on their books and dumped him. After Edwards had finished laughing, Alex prompted him to ask about Eric Cantona. 'OK then, he's yours' says Sgt. Wilko and the deal is done in a trice. A fairly ridiculous scenario to set up the most epochal transfer since Robbo's arrival over a decade before.

JFK's shooting had nothing on this. Where were you when you heard the news? Everyone can recall the shock, the joy and the pure *Schardenfreude* of that moment. Manc phone lines burned hot as the news spread whilst our Yorkie friends were paralysed by the trauma. Let us be honest: few of us had any real idea of what Eric was going to bring us – we may even have had nervous doubts. What was undeniable and utterly delightful was the knowledge that all Leeds would be devastated beyond endurance. The savage outbreak of recrimination, despair and anger in Sheep City was wondrous to behold. This was worse than Revie's death, worse than the '73 Cup

Final, worse than your favourite ewe giving you an STD: all that could be heard from the East was the desolate howling of the betrayed lover.

I'd seen Eric play in France and had long been convinced that he was a Gallic George Best. When he came to England, I longed for him to come to OT but knew that Alex would never countenance such a presence in the dressing-room. I despaired when he settled in Leeds and fully understood the rapture of Elland Road as he unveiled his unparalleled majesty. Leeds fans, for so long the epitome of xenophobic macho-men, became homosexual Francophiles overnight. In a way this was not that surprising. Here was a player of thrilling flair, excitement and glitter-drenched individualism and thus as such was totally alien to Leeds fans; it was akin to showing primitive man fire for the first time. The Sheep duly warmed their genitalia on his incandescence on the pitch and me...I felt as bitter as the most acerbic of Blues.

So as it turned out, there was no marriage between Leeds and Eric, just the briefest of affairs that left the Sheep impotent and frustrated. The spotty, shaven-headed Tyke fan had been granted a few nights with Kim Basinger and had fallen hopelessly in love only to watch in horror as she went off hand-in-hand with the hunk from down the road. Back to the local wildlife for Leeds – the start of a beautiful relationship for the Reds.

Why Eric left Leeds is a question shrouded in mystery and speculation. At the time, unsavoury rumours abounded which tended to refer darkly to 'off-the-field behaviour' – what Private Eye would term 'Ugandan discussions'. Certainly such stories kept Red Issue in jokes about donkeys, sex and housewives for months. When Eric's book came out, he accused Wilko of driving him out with his contradictory comments which left Eric bemused and uncertain of his standing. Wilko struck back in The Sun claiming Eric had forced him to sell and for a while legal action seemed possible. This wasn't even handbags at 10 paces – more pouting at 30 miles. Frankly, who cares? The

French Genius, a supposed *enfant terrible*, became Eric the Red, King of Old Trafford and history was made. Leeds left with piles of Cantona Christmas presents – United left with a superstar, a title and a glorious future.

Perhaps the key to this is understanding that Eric is typically French. Anyone who's studied history knows that for France, glory – *La Gloire* – is all to them. Just winning is not enough; it must be done with style, panache and passion. Why did the French turn out to support Napoleon in such huge numbers when he came back from exile in Elba? Because they wanted glory, even if that meant glorious defeat. How could Leeds ever hope to fulfil this genetic need of Cantona? A club whose greatest moments are only remembered by the rest of the country for their cynicism, negativity, and 'efficiency'? A club whose recent title was won by default from a team they haven't beaten since 1981? A club so unused to flair or style that they left Eric on the bench more often than not?

119

Of course Eric came to us – who else in Britain can claim to have elevated true glory to the highest principle of living? Where else could Eric's existential vision be realised? Eric, an Albert Camus fan, would dismiss any notion of destiny but for those who believe in such things, how obvious that he should've ended up at the Theatre of Dreams. The Sheep were dreaming to think they could hold him there: Elland Road is the last place on Earth for a true artist. Now Brian Deane, well, THAT'S what I call Leeds style.

*   *   *   *   *

Dropping a sparkling star catalyst like Cantona into a team equation does not produce instant combustion, of course. The most perceptive early comment about Eric was from George Best who remarked that Eric had "given the team a brain at last." Naturally it would take a while for this new cerebral presence to mesh into the side, for it to link up the synapses and mainline into the team's nerve centres. You don't turn around teams in an instant – they're more like supertankers, gradually arcing around away from the destination marked 'More Aimless Bollocks' towards the port reserved for Champions. Even so, the rapidity with which United were transformed by Eric's arrival was surely without precedent in our history. We'd thought for months that we needed both a striker and a midfield player; now we had the two – but in one man. Both were the best in Europe.

Eric was to become uncontainable. Whether playing centre-forward banging in volleys and tap-ins inside the box, or as an inside-forward bringing in colleagues by means of a dazzling array of flicks, shimmies and shakes, or as a deep-lying midfield creator dragging dazed defenders into his maze, he won over even the most xenophobically suspicious within weeks. By entrancing us and bewitching his opponents, he also rather pleasingly made complete arseholes of hire-a-mouth rent-a-quotes in the media who played the Cassandra role with such gusto when he arrived. Have the likes of Hansen & Co ever made such disastrously incorrect prognostications?

The last piece of the Championship jigsaw (available at £5.99 in the Superstore, suckers) was slotted into place with the return of Lee Sharpe. Absent for an eternity with meningitis and hernia trouble – and not, as some wags might suggest, as the result of a particularly extended bad trip – the original boy wonder was back to provide the telling crosses that Giggsy was not quite up to supplying. McClair was to move back to midfield wherein his blade-covering toil might find greater effect, to the surprise of the Choccy fan club who'd always claimed he was better right up front. The Premier Eleven was at last in place, with Andrei and Robbo chomping at the bit on the bench, ever ready to pick up the gauntlet when opportunity knocked. (Three clichés in one line – time to apply for a tabloid job.)

With Eric brooding under his eyebrows in the stand, a ready-made replacement for some unfortunate Red, the team squeezed the Arsenal pricks virgin-tight to win 1-0 through Hughesy's goal, the extra edge in our play evident in every quarter. A week before the litmus-test visit of leaders Norwich, City arrived at OT, 700 Bluenoses in tow, to be given a stylish lesson from the Masters of Manchester. McMahon, clearly relishing the chance to renew hostilities with his old enemies, spent the match lumbering around like a toothless, arthritic Rottweiler, utterly outclassed by a tigerish Ince who found himself with enough time on his hands to go forward and score a blinding opener.

Hughes, patently back to his rampaging best, outdid himself by netting a luminous volley of supreme class. City pulled a lucky one back and scrambled around feverishly for the last 10 minutes but Peter ensured no travesty of justice ensued. Reid won the Ronnie Moran award for post-match bullshit, by claiming "...only those two strikes were the difference between the teams" proving only that his advanced state of ageing had atrophied his eyesight.

Against Norwich and a vengeance-seeking Mark Robins,

United simply piled so much pressure on them that no amount of wayward finishing was going to deny us three vital points, Hughes duly completing the job on the hour. Eric began to display the vision and touch that was to illuminate 1993; his first goal came a week later at Stamford Bridge during a bit of an off-day for the team, the memory of which was soon obliterated by the Great Boxing Day Fightback. For many of the thousands of Reds who infiltrated every stand of Hillsborough that day, the game was one of the League highlights of the Fergie Years thus far.

After seven minutes, we appeared to be facing a holiday meltdown of QPR proportions, two behind before we'd even woken up. It seemed symbolic that this United side did what the one of 12 months previous could not – continue to play football, fight and overcome. As the hour approached we had created a slew of chances, three corkers falling to McClair who blew them all, with Sharpe cracking over crosses with the frequency of a serving machine. Unbelievably, Wednesday scored again, leaving us 25 minutes to pull back three. Somehow, United found an extra gear, an extra yard, an extra zest for the fight that no team who are three down has the right to expect. McClair belatedly refixed his sights, scored twice in 13 minutes as Sharpe began to take the left-sided piss until Eric stumbled the equaliser into the net.

It was some measure of the maelstrom United had whipped up that we were baying for a winner as the whistle went, the Owls crumpling in relief that they'd been spared the final sword thrust. The euphoria all at United felt was entirely understandable; not only had we retrieved an impossible situation but more importantly we'd seen the first full flowering of the United creation machine. This was a side that appeared to be balanced, in tune and endlessly resourceful, able to carve openings at will with the precision and incision of surgeons but done with the speed, passion and fight demanded by Red Devil tradition. Over the next 23 days, we demonstrated this to the outside world to devastating effect – Fergie's six years of alchemic experiment had finally melded mortal individuals into a team of immortal achievement.

Two days after Hillsborough, the first half-decent Coventry side in living memory turned up at OT, fresh from inflicting a 5-1 humiliation on Liverpool and a 3-0 win over title-pretenders Aston Villa. On a freezing afternoon, with hundreds locked out and anticipation at frenzied levels, United served up a banquet to satisfy the palate of the pickiest gourmet. Those who'd had to shell out £80 plus for touted tickets were rewarded by five goals and a display of peacock-strutting arrogance from a team that had found its self-belief. Eric, a football *auteur* if ever there was one, wrote the script and directed the action; if Ince and Giggs were the stars, Irwin's cameo role in the 84th minute provided the performance's defining moment.

Bypassing the FA Cup sideshow with a nod to Phelan and young Gillespie for their goals in a second-gear win, the visit of Spurs, always a glamour game in itself, became a glitter-spangled celebration. Providing us with a sterner test than Coventry by defending in depth, Spurs at first plunged us into a familiar scenario – a team beating its head against a wall, a crowd becoming increasingly nervy and impatient. In '91/'92, such a game could easily have finished goal-less or worse. Now, the inclusion of Eric gave us a centre of calm authority at the heart of the side, also able to produce the momentary inspirations on which games turn. Such was his looping Strettie header before half-time, soothing the fevered brows of fans and players alike. Nevertheless that scarcely prepared us for the second half sunburst.

There are generally two ways of giving opponents a good duffing up. The first is the one employed against Coventry – a general overwhelming dominance that dripfeeds goals at steady intervals throughout the game, the sort of thing Liverpool used to specialise in, although only when playing rubbishy teams of course. The second method is perhaps more United's style, a pattern that we've now become accustomed to and even *blasé* about – the one in which the team suddenly transforms the pace and power of their play, burns incandescently with passion and commitment and then, in a short-time frame, proceeds to wipe the opposition off the face of the planet.

These 10 to 20 minute explosions that might reap two, three or four goals produce an intensity of emotion and excitement that nothing in life can quite match. You are left reeling from the repeated adrenalin surges, dizzy in the delirium induced by the ceaseless flow of attacks and chances that pause for neither breath nor reply. It may well have been preceded by half-an-hour of cautious probing and low-level skirmishing: once the climax is spent, it may well be followed by mere piss-taking and arrogant possession football. Despite that 'waste' of match-time, it's worth it – the experience of that spell of pure wonder remains imprinted on your consciousness forever. Why can't you forget that 10 minute spell against Liverpool in '89? Because when you live through something of that intensity, it never leaves you. When United turn it on like they did after half-time against Spurs and you add that memory to your collection of the most life-enhancing United moments, you can feel justified for once in the ridiculous amount of time and money you devote through the years to United – for where else can you get that sort of visceral thrill? Nowhere, mate.

Within an eight minute spell, Denis, Choccy and, incredibly, Paul Parker scored. These weren't just goals but slices of pure unalloyed wizardry, magic that mere video-tape and TV replays cannot fully express. Eric's sorceror's touch for Irwin's demonic finish, the way McClair's thunderbolt sparkled through the air and the sheer insouciance of Parker's trip the light fantastic were sights that would befit heaven. Surely every one of the 35,600 who were there knew that they'd witnessed something special.

No wonder that there were 9,000 Reds at Loftus Road for a Monday night match that was live on Sky. Who would dare risk missing a repeat performance? Presumably QPR had long since realised that there was no way they would be able to hold even a Cantona-less United because they spent much of the match attempting to separate limbs from United torsos. Alan MacDonald set a disgraceful captain's example by booting Hughes off the pitch after 12 minutes, somehow escaping a red card; Parker was later appallingly scythed down the leg by sad Skinner-lookalike Sinton, giving Sky viewers an unexpected glimpse of the body's inner workings. It was turning into an episode of *Jimmy's* out there but United refused to descend to Rangers' debased standards. Ince, utterly masterful in his role as the team's fulcrum, netted a remarkable overhead kick; Giggs made a complete fool of the QPR defence for the second. Following QPR's scarcely deserved reply, Andrei seized his first team chance to rifle home a dazzling third having roared down the pitch like a MiG at take-off. Cue the Cossack dance song – United were back at the top of the League.

Thus passed the greatest spell of the season, the tastiest expression of the '93 United vintage. A four hour tape of Coventry and QPR, with the 20 minute bursts from Norwich away and Spurs, would suffice to demonstrate to any doubter that United, at their best, were truly unbeatable and the worthiest of Champs. True, exactly 12 months before, we'd also hit a seasonal peak; in the months to come we would sporadically face the same accusations that we were in decline or, ugh, 'losing our bottle'. But this United was older, wiser and better – and in Ince and Cantona, had genius that would not be denied its rightful place at the top.

Although it's hard to forgive Forest for all the transfer stitch-ups in the past, for knocking us out of the Cup in '89 and for employing a major Red-hater as manager for so long, it's equally hard not to appreciate the fact that they do at least come to play football at OT, unlike the defeat-fearing wimps of Leeds, Ipswich and Arsenal *et al.* The 2-0 victory was wrought from a game distinguished by the players' intelligence, skill and imagination, rightly crowned by an unforgettable Hughes strike of lightning. Forest fans chanting "We're going down –

you're not" were applauded by K-Stand, Choccy's shock star performance perhaps having gone to their head.

We then lost at Portman Road after Schmeichel got caught in quicksanded no-man's land but even this 2-1 reverse couldn't dampen the soaring Red spirits. It must have been the most generously received United defeat in years. United's fightback, which came within a goalie's leg of saving a point, was continually inspired by the longest rendition of 'Fergie's Red & White Army' ever heard. It left the Ipswich support open-mouthed in admiration. For once, United seemed to have made some friends, as we discovered the following year.

February '92 had been the moment when it all began to fall apart for the BC United, when tension gripped the loins and lost points were scattered to the winds. February '93 could so easily have taken us down that miserable path to purgatory; at home to both Sheff. Utd and the Saints, we exhibited the same symptoms. Too many players on off-days, a slack goal down and a crowd feasting on fingernails – but this time the gods, in the form of their earthly representatives Cantona and Giggs, were to be kinder. In '92 when the chips were down, no saviours would appear in a puff of penalty box smoke to save the day; this year it seemed there would always be one Red shirted hero prepared to take up the challenge and rescue us all. Against the Blades, Eric made Choccy's goal and then volleyed the winner, his first for United, into the Paddock goal with nine minutes left. He rose up in front of us and we adored Him. Dave Basset said later that Eric was "nothing special – I'd buy others before him." Sheffield United are now in the Endsleigh League. Can you spot the connection there readers?

Against the Saints, deliverance was even more dramatic. With eight minutes left, the ghost of George Best entered Ryan Giggs, took him into the box for two virtual one-on-ones and left Flowers on his humiliated arse as the second-greatest living Welshman peeled away to celebrate (these being the days when Ryan still deigned to show joy upon scoring brilliant goals). Of course, it was utterly undeserved, unexpected and unfair –

precisely the sort of miraculous turn of events that can convince the most hardened pessimist that the title was heading west to us.

Naturally, this was the one sentiment you could not under any circumstances express publicly at any Red gathering. It was by now a stadium rule that no song could be sung or even whispered that invoked any mention whatsoever of 'championships'. Deafening volleys of "Shhh!" would greet any ignorant soul who ventured down that avenue. Over-confidence or cockiness were certainly no part of the '93 *zeitgeist* – after last season's trauma, the only permissible attitude was "Prepare for the worst – pray for the best." Obviously this collective mindset had a bit of inhibitory effect on the atmosphere at OT; it's hard to loosen the vocal chords when, metaphorically, you've got your fingers up your rectum to stop you crapping yourself. Being one down in the last 10 minutes at home to some duffers when you're in a three-way title race is, surely, one of life's more stressful experiences. Weight loss through anxiety was the only beneficial aspect of this situation, although Pete Boyle seemed to have missed this one. (Incidentally, it was around this time that Pete, the Burnage Bard of OT, made his fateful drunken promise to streak at Selhurst should United win the title. What might he have planned for a win in Europe? You shudder at the possibilities...)

The 'West Stand' had by now begun to rise prominently from the rubble of the Strettie and was filled with sodden pack-a-mackers; when it rained we looked like a parade of freshly-withdrawn condomed willies at an orgy. Despite barbed comments from K-Stand, they were quite good times in there, considering the circumstances, as a camaraderie of a sort developed, united as we were by an inferiority complex and raging paranoia in general. And being 10 yards from Giggsy when he buried the second against the Saints made up for much.

February's awaydays meant two trips to Yorkshire. A Cup defeat at Bramhall Lane despite Giggsy's oft-replayed opener came courtesy of yet another United penalty fiasco; the hard-faced objective truth was that it was better for us to go out but that was scant solace for the thousands behind the goal as Brucey blew out. The previous Monday, we took our lives in our hands to trek to Elland Road, there to witness first-hand the full existential crisis of the bestial Tykes. Since our last visit, they had lost Eric, of course; they had also been exposed as one-season wonders and been forced to watch United getting tooled up to raid their trophy-room for the title.

They offered their usual animalistic welcome; 300 shrieking specimens of scumbaggery surrounded the United coach to vent their bile at Eric. Inside the ground, any declared Red ran the habitual risk of GBH from the pondlife in white; 30,000 purple-faced plonkers howled hysterically every time Eric touched the ball. In the run-up to the game, *Red Issue* had provided a paper aeroplane cut-out to be thrown at the Leeds hordes which thanked LUFC for selling us Eric. What a sweet gesture from the well-brought up fanzine boys, you might think. Sadly, Leeds reacted badly to this expression of grati-tude; United Supporters' Clubs were asked to prevent these missives from being delivered for fear they might offend.

What Barry Moorhouse was doing kow-towing to those onanists I do not know. No effort was expended to minimise the offence to Reds caused by the Munich T-shirts and songs that night, so why on earth should we be tiptoeing around Leeds' finer sensibilities in such a craven way? In the end, the Club's attempt at appeasement – which as any historian knows is NOT the way to deal with aggressive fascist types anyway – completely failed; even Sky TV were forced to comment on the shower of paper planes that filled the air. The game finished goal-less, Schmeichel redeeming himself for Portman Road and Leeds' success-free run against us continued unmolested. Which is more than can be said for the local ewes.

The month ended with a satisfactory dispatch of Middles-boro to whence they came, Giggsy's continued brilliance com-pensating for the poor form of Lee Sharpe. We wondered what

Andrei had to do to get a game; as in '91/'92, it appeared he just wasn't one of Fergie's favourites. We now know that Andrei twice asked for transfers before last season, understandably frustrated by his lengthy spells of bench-warming – shades of the Jesper 'Judge' Olsen syndrome – and by the sight of players retaining their places despite prolonged spells of indifference. In fact, Sharpe didn't really come good again until well into April. David Meek lectured us about Sharpe's status as the King of the Assists but the truth was that those had mainly come before mid-January. Andrei just had to accept that Lee had joined Choccy in the Fergie-adopted-son club and had to take his chances when the absences of others allowed.

One of those chances was at Liverpool; Eric was out for two games. For 20 minutes, our defence fell apart in front of a pumped up Kop; then came Peter's Banksian save from Hutchinson and the game turned on that sixpence. Paul Stewart, the Bluenose reject, helpfully fed Denis to set up Hughesy's goal; Rush's equaliser was simply brushed aside by a swaggering United, McClair netting the easiest header imaginable within smelling distance of the stinking Kop sewer. It could have finished three or four; sweet revenge for April, naturally, but also richly emblematic of the shift in football's balance of power. From now on, United were the undisputed Kings of the North while Liverpool, sinking into trophy-less mediocrity, were the ones who would be treating the clash of the Reds as their seasonal cup final. The roles of the '80s had been neatly reversed – long may it continue thus.

Incidentally, how nice of so many Scousers to, presumably, sell their tickets to Reds, allowing us to take over huge tracts of the Main and Centenary Stands. Given the amount of support 'Pool got from their own fans, the rest might as well have stayed away too. With any luck, now that the Kop has been demolished, Anfield will become the most easily outsung crowd in the Premiership.

The only sour note, apart from the odd flurry of heroin-stained fists from Scousers aggrieved to find Reds next to them, was the *Sunday Mirror*'s report of the one minute's silence for Tony Bland. Alone amongst the press, the *Mirror* inflated the figure of a half-dozen disruptors to 'hundreds', establishing yet another myth for our rivals to exploit. The *Mirror*, arguably the worst Sunday paper and currently sporting rapidly declining sales, was part of the Maxwell stable, as was *The People*; Fergie accused that august organ of being the highest producer of United-related fantasy stories in Fleet Street. What is it about these two? Has working for the Bouncing Czech perverted their sense of truth so much that they have lost all understanding of what facts are? For the record, the disruption was minimal; indeed Liverpudlians were quoted as being grateful for the respectful response.

* * * * *

The tabloid press continued to display their disfigured sense of reality in March, whipping up a 'bottle crisis at United' story out of next to nothing, clearly salivating rabidly at the thought that the Reds might be derailed once more. True enough, we dropped six points in four games but reading the reports of the games you'd seen, you could only wonder what planet the hacks had been on during the 90 minutes. According to them, we were losing the plot, losing our bottle and losing the title; the ghosts of '92 were rising out of the pitch to claim the life of another Red season. What is it about United and the month of March anyway? Five seasons running, March has seen our League form take a dip. That soothsayer of Julius Caesar's knew his stuff all right.

Fair enough, the defeat up at Oldham's Ice Station Zebra was faintly embarrassing but the performance four days later in the six-pointer against Villa hardly warranted the gloomy prophesying of the press blood-hounds. A splendid match on a golden afternoon beamed live all over Europe as an advertisement for the English game – stuff your Calcio Italia or Bundesliga tank manoeuvres – admittedly should have been won; we made at least 15 clear chances and on any other day might have scored a hatful.

As it was, Staunton managed to avoid heat exhaustion, dehydration and sunburn long enough to score a floored-jaw opener. For once, OT recalled its '70s pedigree, creating an instant, ever-expanding swarming swell of noise until, as the cacophony climaxed, Hughes thundered his Paddock header homewards. We stayed top on goal difference – 61 points from 33 games with Norwich perched potentially on 59. Sure, we'd dropped points but we'd settle for displays like that every week for eternity. At a strangely subdued Maine Road, two more dropped points but no sign of '92-style panic or despondency. Blues kidded themselves that they could have won it but in truth were spared by United's profligacy. The goals highlighted the gulf in class between '90s City and United; theirs a typical beanpole Wimblearse special, ours a stunningly sweet move capped by a majestic header by Eric, the sort of goal City could only dream of seeing from a Blueshirt.

Then, midweek, Arsenal brought their smothering blanket defence and their second rate support whose only song appeared to be 'You'll Never Win the League'. As if the Gunners will ever win it again with such a negative, soul-destroying side, unless they intend to bore opponents into submission. They are late '60s Leeds in yellow shirts, a team for supporters who don't actually like football very much, the Dire Straits of the Premiership. Of course, the game ended 0-0, what else? Streaming out at full-time, the night was transformed by the result from the south – Norwich had beaten Villa 1-0. It seemed that Ron's boys had been so busy mouthing off about the possibility of United losing their bottle they'd forgotten to keep a grip on their own. I don't know what that did for the players but for us, the trip to Carrow Road on the evening of April 5th couldn't pass quick enough. Hindsight is a wonderful thing but despite the press setting up the match as a floodlit High Noon, the pre-match vibe was sensational; there was none of the gut-wrenching paranoid pessimism of the '92 trip, just a feverent belief that we would teach the nation a lesson.

Everything about that night has passed into folklore and rightly so. Given the circumstances, the title-challenging opposition, the lack of Hughes and the media hype, for United to have emerged with such a Busbyesque display of rampant, ruthless, ravaging attack was almost beyond belief. For those of us who'd stood through the Fergie F*ckwit Years, pockmarked by caution, uncertainty and defensive defeatism, this was the height of exultation. At last we had a team, and presumably a manager, tapped into the true spirit of United – the spirit that had won the last title by winning 6-1 at Upton Park and had turned over Barca in '84. The eight minute supernova of goals bettered even that we'd seen against Spurs and in Andrei's goal, we saw perhaps the most sublime move of the season.

We'd not only buried Norwich on the night, we'd destroyed their season; the self-belief that flowed through the team from that moment on took us forward through the title-winning run of seven straight wins. Were there ever such exuberant renditions of the 'Cossack Dance' and the 'Marseillaise' in history? Robbo came on to an outbreak of Wayne's World genuflections, an entirely fitting entrance on the night United took their giant step towards mission accomplished. Next day, the press scrambled madly to shower us with every superlative at their command – there was to be no more talk of bottle until the champagne was uncorked in May.

If that had been the greatest awayday of '93, we had only to wait until Saturday for the home highspot. What a week that was to be a Red. Against Sheffield Wednesday for 86 minutes or so, Old Trafford was in a timewarp, back in Easter '92, roasting hot and being done to a turn by Forest; an hour and a half of *déjà vu.* That Bruce of all people should save the game with minutes to go created pandemonium enough; that he should again head a *winner* in the depths of injury-time was a miracle of Biblical proportions.

They say the British and Mancunians in particular are a reserved sub-species but at that moment 40,000 lost every inhibition they had. Never in the field of human conflict have so many blokes kissed so many others in so few minutes. Alex and Kiddo staged an impromtu pitch invasion; Barry Davies' voice reached pre-pube pitch; a vision of the Premiership trophy flashed in front of a million Red eyes. After the whistle, the Main Stand outside concourse filled with pure delirium, Reds screaming with delight into each other's faces, unwilling to go home, in fact barely able to move so transfixed with ecstasy were we. Although you still didn't dare say it out loud, surely you knew in your bones that this was it at last.

The rest of the run-in tumbled by in a cascade of mounting excitement, anticipation and alcoholic frenzy as the Reds powered towards the finishing post. The Red Army assembled to invade and annex Highfield Road and see Denis win the game; Chelsea were imperiously dismissed at OT amidst the most light-headed, tension-free atmosphere at the ground that season. At Selhurst Park, the untold thousands of Reds banked around the ground revelled in the news of Villa's 3-0 defeat at Ewood as the team took to the field for the second half. Hughesy's volley was spectacularly befitting what was, in effect, a title-winning goal, his face as he roared away a picture of fulfilment – don't you just love the way he seems to bellow to the heavens when he scores particularly epochal goals? Even more apt that it should be a Cantona-Ince combination that sealed the game, our two best players of '93 taking the final bow.

Sunday afternoon, May 2nd 1993. A Liverpool-supporting Scouser scores Oldham's winner at Villa Park live on Sky. United are the Champions, 24 hours before what could have been a tough match against Blackburn. I'm not even going to attempt to write anything about the 36 hours that followed. Every Red knows what winning the title meant to us; every Red has his own special memories of those days that count as among the greatest in our lives. In fact, I defy anyone to be able to put into words how it felt and what it meant. As for the Blackburn game, you were either there, in which case any description would be unnecessary or you weren't in which case any description would be inadequate. It's hard to encapsulate the emotional impact the title win had on every Red; will there ever be anything quite like it again? Perhaps only winning the European Cup will match it and even that's not for sure. All I can say is thank God I was born a Red and lived long enough to be there.

*   *   *   *   *

RED-EYE

"I've lived in Oz for 14 years but the day Villa lost to Oldham I said to my wife 'I've got to see the Reds at Wimbledon.' In three days, I'd got myself a passport and a stand-by ticket. I finally managed to get on a flight to Singapore on the Friday – it was going to be cutting it fine. Anyway, by Saturday night I'm in Kuala Lumpar, trying to get a flight to England with kick off 15 hours away. I'm in this toilet in the middle of nowhere and I look up and I nearly wet myself on the spot – written in big, fresh letters is '18 Years and Won Fuck All, City is Our Name'! Just a perfect moment! I got to Selhurst in the end, paid a tout 20 quid to stand behind the goal. When I finally got back to Oz, I formed the West Australia MUSC, 80 members already; we spend all our time watching Reds vids and getting pissed. And my wife thought I'd got it all out of my system!"

Jim Dickenson (ex-Wythenshawe) Perth W.A.

*   *   *   *   *

134

25,000 Reds turned up for a second party at Selhurst Park which got slightly derailed by a pitch invasion but which at least afforded Pete Boyle the opportunity to prove he was a man of his word with his 'wand'. This magical season was over. Wasn't that summer the best in living memory?

* * * * *

Within hours of the Sunday's final whistle at Villa Park, the floodgates opened nationally with spectacular effect. Just as we were finally able to yell "Champions!" for hours on end after weeks of not daring even to *think* the word, the media cut loose with the relieved abandon of the post-laxative constipated. Months of stories about title tension and bottle could be forgotten; editors could now sit back allow their front pages and bulletins to blare 'Man United – f*cking great or what?'

TV specials, newspaper pull-outs, souvenir editions, new United magazines, picture portfolios, special United offers and endless media items covering every conceivable United angle filled the summer months. Frankly, it was incredible – the most sustained media footie hype since 1968. To be honest, a lot of it was tacky and even embarrassing but at least it had the gratifying effect of making the recess unbearable for our Bitter, Scouse and Sheepy friends who were unable to open a paper without seeing Ryan Giggs' smouldering features or a picture of the gleaming, Red-bedecked Premiership crown.

The scintillating form of the team after the August restart simply exacerbated the situation beyond the control of the Club; an entire United industry has grown up, churning out endless product lines for the voracious masses. United penetrated every corner of national life; the players were becoming as nationally and internationally famous as the England '66 team. Eric Cantona: feted as a genius *non pareil*. Giggs: female Britain's sex god, getting more fan mail than Take That and Bad Boys Inc. combined. Fergie: talked of in reverential tones not heard since Shankly's halcyon days. When even Steve Bruce's distorted facial features start adorning teenage walls, it's clear something remarkable is happening.

Football as a sport has, of course, become remarkably trendy since Italia '90 and *World In Motion*. Liverpool in '85 had done more than most to put the game in the cultural doghouse but Gazza and Co had secured its rehabilitation. The groundwork had been accomplished before 1990, thanks to the fanzines, the crossover between music and footie in the late '80s of which *World In Motion* (written by United fans New Order) was a product and the 'death' of hooliganism – Italia '90 just provided the final, nationwide shared catharsis that sealed the transformation. Not only did the lads come back to the game but they brought with them their sisters, girlfriends and mates. The feminisation of fandom had begun; with it, a heightened sense of fashionability.

In retrospect, it should have been obvious that the first truly great post-'90 team was going to reap a sensational harvest of support now that Britain had a pro-football culture once more. Arsenal were non-starters for obvious reasons; nothing as boring, ugly and unglamorous as that lot could ever be linked to ANY concept of trendiness. Leeds were equally charisma-free and as back-door Champions who were then utterly unable to mount a defence, too glory-free to qualify. United have stepped in and cleaned up; already steeped in glamour, with young, hip players and a style that exudes grace, power and visceral excitement – we fit the bill to perfection. As *The Guardian* noted before anyone else, in the wake of England's turnip disaster, United have to many people become 'the national side'. At the same time, thanks to Giggs, Sharpe, Eric and Pally (apparently), United have also become, if you follow the analogy of football as the new Rock 'n' Roll, the Beatles/Take That/Duran Duran of soccer. United are trendiness in shorts and the girls 'n' boys love us.

The 'female aspect' of this development has not found favour with everyone; I shan't repeat here the terrace joke about United, fishy smells and being followed by pussy. The well-founded suspicion is that once Giggs leaves/grows a beard/sleeps with Incey, the hordes of teenage girls will desert United in droves and latch on to, say, Jamie Redknapp or some other smooth-jawed *Just Seventeen* dreamboat. Some are embarrassed by the introduction of pop star-fan shenanigans into what is, after all, a sport club – just as many of the '60s faithful found the Best phenomenon a bit off. Others simply just can't accept teenybopper girlies at footie matches in the first place. Frankly, having seen what happened to Bros, Curiosity *et al*, you can't blame the lads for being wary; if these girls are still there when we're struggling at Wimbledon on a wet Wednesday with Giggs injured sometime in the future, then hats off all-round to them.

As for the general surge in new support for United – and leaving aside the 'Mancs v The Rest' aspects of this – perhaps we should stop grumbling about bandwagon jumpers and welcome this historic opportunity to change the nature of footie-following population forever. Undoubtedly, part-timers and day-trippers are there to be sneered at but surely most of the new Reds will turn out to be true to the core. The thousands of pre-teens who are now pledging their allegiance to us are the guarantors of our future glory. Whole regions in the west of Lancashire, for example, which were Liverpool for a decade will be turning Devil Red over the next few years as current kids become teenagers and take over the streets. This is the greatest spin off from May '93 – welcome it!

Elsewhere in 1992/93

◻ Vinny 'Mosquito Brain' Jones gets a £20,000 fine for his part in the 'Hard Men' video; by that token, we suggest Danny Baker gets six months for his aggravating efforts.

◻ Gazza is in trouble again after belching into a TV microphone; the Italians fail to understand that, for a Geordie, this constitutes an intellectual comment.

◻ Leeds embarrass English football by losing the Battle of Britain Euro clash with Rangers; thereafter they plummet to the foot of the table. Such worthy Champions.

◻ City get slaughtered in the much-hyped FA Cup tie with Spurs and promptly invade the pitch; in an outbreak of Scouse disease they try to suggest that it wasn't their fault. The FA let City off; Peter Swales was Chairman of the FA Committee. Surprise, surprise.

◻ Brain Clough, amidst allegations of drunkenness and ticket touting, quits Forest, having led them to relegation. How sad.

◻ United fans campaign to 'Save Our Souness' succeeds as Anfield announces he's staying on. For some reason, Graeme omits to thank us...

◻ Sugar and Venables fall out at Spurs; allegations about dodgy practices soon follow. Tel later gets the England job, beating off applications from Ronnie Biggs, Arthur Daley and the Krays.

1993/94

The trouble with success is that it leaves you with nothing to complain about; for a city that produced Albert Tatlock and Percy Sugden, this is a grievous state of affairs. From the outset of the new season, things looked grim for those of us who like a good moan. The successful signing of Roy Keane was a blatant disregard of OT tradition – i.e. that every summer, United must fail to buy the best on offer, preferably as a result of Boardroom stinginess. Damian apparently turned down a better deal from Blackburn to join us and the PLC made a record sum of £3.75 million available to get him. Outrageous!

More promising for the whingers was the announcement of a new away kit but even this turned sour when it became clear that the black strip was the last word in cool and damn lucky for the team to boot. The final insult was United's early season form: instead of the usual stumbling start, bizarre player selections and defensive drowsiness, we got perfect tactics, thrilling games and an array of dazzling goals. Even the one subject guaranteed to get us growling – Choccy and where he should play – was removed from the debating arena by virtue of Alex turfing him out of the first 11. It all took some getting used to for Reds accustomed to apoplexy and apprehension – life was just too perfect.

Our rivals contributed to this amazing state of unreality by falling apart at refreshingly regular intervals. Leeds spent the year flailing about pathetically, trying to convince themselves that Brian Deane was an adequate replacement for Eric the King, hitting the headlines only when their bestial support disgraced themselves live on TV or when being dumped out of the Cup by nobodies from the sticks. City turned their years of bitterness on themselves, pursuing Swales, his board, his mother and his wig mercilessly until he finally quit, whilst watching surely the worst-ever football seen at the Moss Side Slum. Liverpool enjoyed the fruits of the Sourness rebuilding project which entailed watching an Endsleigh-standard team become the nation's laughing stock, the moribund Kop stunned into silence by the atrocities being committed by the carthorses on the pitch.

The only club offering us any sort of challenge was to be Blackburn. There, at least, was something over which to fulminate. A small-town, small-time club, their glories long since faded, rejuvenated by a capitalist sugar-daddy who was ready to pay anything to assemble a winning team. Blackburn players essentially play the role of whoring tarts, happy to take the money and dance for their big boy boss, ignoring the fact that the majority of their supporters are United-hating band-waggoners who'll flee back to Anfield should tough times return.. They are an example of the worst feature of modern football – the artificial club, entirely dependant on the whim of some moneyed baron who's made his pile from depriving workers of their rightful share, a team that would disintegrate in a trice if they were forced to live off their supporters like the rest of us.

Clubs like Blackburn, Parma and Monaco are a stain on the soul of football, the Western equivalent of the old Eastern Bloc clubs like Dinamo Berlin and Steaua Bucharest who survived and succeeded only through the patronage of the *apparatchiks* of the ruling Commie parties. To those who defend Walker's bankrolling as "good for the game" because it injects new money into football, learn some economics. All Blackburn's spending does is produce rampant football inflation, jacking up transfer fees and forcing competing clubs to break their wage structures with the net result that we fans end up spending more to keep the same football industry in luxury. You can only hope that another stock market crash is due soon and that Walker will lose every penny.

141

The Blackburn challenge, however, didn't materialise for a good five months. Within weeks of the Charity Shield, in which United at last won a penalty shoot-out in front of a Red-dominated crowd (where were Arsenal? Too far to travel was it?), it became clear that United weren't just head and shoulders above the rest but into the stratosphere and out of sight. With the title win, the weight built up over 26 years had been lifted from the shoulders leaving the team free to express their brilliance to us all. You had to get your head around the truth that we were now the undisputed best, not just a good team capable of beating anyone on their day or one of the leading pack but simply the best. You also had to get used to the change in style the team's new self-confidence had effected.

We were now able to shift gears and change the pace at will, our defence arrogant enough to soak up the opposition's feeble attempts at penetration until our forwards fancied a bit of sport. After years in which our teams only knew one tune, we could now transform ourselves into the most demonic counter-attacking band whenever necessary. The quicksilver pace, telepathic understanding and world-class skill that we had in attack was uncontainable and exhilarating. We had reached football Valhalla – a marriage of the awesome efficiency of '70s Leeds or '80s Liverpool with the buccaneering flair of Doc and Busby Uniteds past. The rest looked on in fear and admiration.

Even now, I don't think we've fully taken in the purring premier class football we saw that season. If you listed all the moves and goals that United produced, the proportion that would deserve the title 'outstanding' would dwarf that of any other year since the '60s. Every week, the moments that TV would droolingly replay, analyse and celebrate would habitually be United's; every month seemed to produce a worthy candidate for Goal of the Season, every match a move fit for a contemporary art award. It is said that United as a team were over-hyped; in all honesty, it would be impossible to over-praise much of our football. A City-supporting relative in a drunken moment admitted to me after the Cup Final that

United had played the best football that season he'd seen in 30 years. I congratulated him on a rare display of good judgement. Surely he was right.

* * * * *

With little to complain about on the pitch, frustrated Reds turned to some familiar subjects for some extended scab-picking and navel-gazing. A letter in *Red Issue* from the amusing and redoubtable J.Reeve (of Cheadle Hulme, natch) split open the old debate of Mancs vs non-Mancs and received an avalanche of raging replies from hurt-out-of-towners. No doubt Bluenoses were delighted by this, having peddled the myth of a Blue Manchester for the last decade, this being about the only argument open to them after 18 years of failure. None of this is new, of course, merely being an updated version of the Cockneys vs Mancs disputes of the '70s.

Really, it was all rather tiresome; isn't it regrettable that instead of celebrating our unique ability to garner support from every corner of the globe, we should in effect collaborate with our enemies' attempts to portray us as an Army of gloryhunters? The facts are plain enough. City are unable to get anyone from outside Moss Side to support them for obvious reasons – that they are habitually crap, have virtually no history of glorious endeavour and don't represent any particular tradition of football. Secondly, even if all non-Mancs were expelled from the United Brotherhood we would still fill OT every week. Thirdly, Manchester itself is still and always has been a predominantly Red city. Why else do United zines and merchandise outsell City's so easily inside Manchester? Why is it that walking down Market Street you will see more United tops in 10 minutes than you'll see City tops in an entire afternoon? Why did a newspaper survey inside Manchester discover 50% more Reds than Blues in the city? The truth is that inside and outside Manchester, Reds are dominant and no amount of Bittermen myth-making can alter that reality.

As for the relative splendours of being a Manc or non-Manc

Red, why can't both sides accept the obvious? That is that outsiders are just as capable of being devoted, loyal Red Army troops – it's just that to be a Red AND a a Manc makes you doubly lucky. All of us in this specially-blessed category can revel in our elevated state of grace but there's no need to denigrate fellow Reds merely because they've suffered the misfortune of not being born or bred a Mancunian.

Perhaps what the ethnic-cleansers really had in their sights were the out-of-town, post-'93 bandwaggoners who've played such a reprehensible part in damaging the OT atmosphere. That, at least, is fair enough. The atmos question gave Reds another outlet for spleen venting as the implications of a superbowl stadium sunk in; the failure of the Leeds flag-day, shown up by the Kop's display three days later, seemed to sum up the malaise. Not that the home crowd didn't have its moments – the Norwich and Xmas games roused us sufficiently to trouble the decibel meters. But in general, there was no escaping the fact that the hard-core Reds were creating more noise away than the 40,000 were at home. Worse than that, some elements were importing wholly disgusting practices as witnessed against Chelsea when pockets of 'supporters' de-cided to boo the team off and whinge about their wasted ticket money. It's bad enough that these people choose not to sing but when they start that sort of behaviour, who can blame the rest of us for wanting them out?

K-Stand, the Paddock and the new Strettie engaged in a war of words over who was letting the side down, each claiming to be the centre of vocal support and charging the rest with being thermos-toting Trappists. Naturally, the truth was that every section had its day – although K-Stand not as often as they liked to think – but there was no consistency. This is hardly surprising given that non-LMTBs never know where they're going to be and who'll be next to them. It's true that the overall number of non-singers has increased, a predictable result of the new football environment; it's also true that the death of the terrace, the stewarding and the lack of unreserved seating have all been contributory factors. But surely there is still hope?

Most of the trouble has been caused by the upheaval and dislocation of the rebuilding. Established centres of support have been carved up and thrown around the stadium. The new OT simply hasn't had the chance to 'settle down' yet. Now that the last seats are down, let us hope the thousands of us who are prepared to get behind the lads can sort things out to our advantage – there are still enough of us to do it. By the time this book comes out, maybe the new East Lower will have stepped in to fill the breech? Maybe the burgeoning cluster of mad Reds in the West Upper will continue to thrive and lead the Stretford End out of the Valley of the Thermos? Perhaps the return of the Pete Boyle Choir to K-Stand will kick-start their revival? All is not yet lost. As Ian Brown said, it's not where you're from, it's where you're at – whether you're a Manc or not, an old warrior or a new Red, as long as you open your throat and sing your heart out for the lads, surely you are to be welcomed at OT with the most open of arms.

* * * * *

By Christmas, United were so far ahead in the table that the bookies stopped taking bets. The team had turned into a sleek match-play machine, cruising around effortlessly before switching on the after-burner to torch opponents to death. The only criticism you could level at them was over-confident complacency which occasionally cost a couple of points; Newcastle and Norwich were amongst the lucky beneficiaries. So, of course, were G*l*t*s*r*y, but in this house, we don't talk about the '94 Euro Cup. Ever. (If you're determined to relive the nightmare, check out Jim White's excellent tome 'Are You Watching Liverpool?')

At a couple of half-time intervals, you might grumble that United had clearly spent the first half pissing about and that you could have had longer in the pub but after the break, they'd come out and make it up to you; Spurs and QPR were amongst

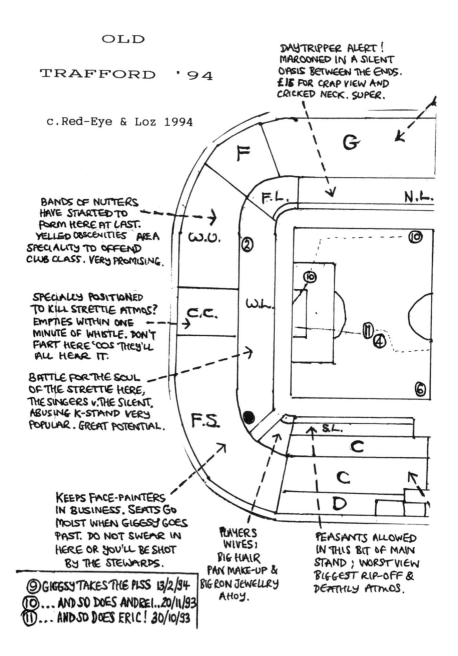

OLD

TRAFFORD '94

c.Red-Eye & Loz 1994

DAY TRIPPER ALERT! MAROONED IN A SILENT OASIS BETWEEN THE ENDS. £15 FOR CRAP VIEW AND CRICKED NECK. SUPER.

BANDS OF NUTTERS HAVE STARTED TO FORM HERE AT LAST. YELLED OBSCENITIES AREA SPECIALITY TO OFFEND CLUB CLASS. VERY PROMISING.

SPECIALLY POSITIONED TO KILL STRETLE ATMOS? EMPTIES WITHIN ONE MINUTE OF WHISTLE. DON'T FART HERE 'COS THEY'LL ALL HEAR IT.

BATTLE FOR THE SOUL OF THE STRETLE HERE, THE SINGERS v. THE SILENT. ABUSING K-STAND VERY POPULAR. GREAT POTENTIAL.

KEEPS FACE-PAINTERS IN BUSINESS. SEATS GO MOIST WHEN GIGGSY GOES PAST. DO NOT SWEAR IN HERE OR YOU'LL BE SHOT BY THE STEWARDS.

PLAYERS WIVES; BIG HAIR PAN MAKE-UP & BIG RON JEWELLRY AHOY.

PEASANTS ALLOWED IN THIS BIT OF MAIN STAND; WORST VIEW BIGGEST RIP-OFF & DEATHLY ATMOS.

⑨ GIGGSY TAKES THE PISS 13/2/94
⑩ ... AND SO DOES ANDREI ..20/11/93
⑪ ... AND SO DOES ERIC! 30/10/93

146

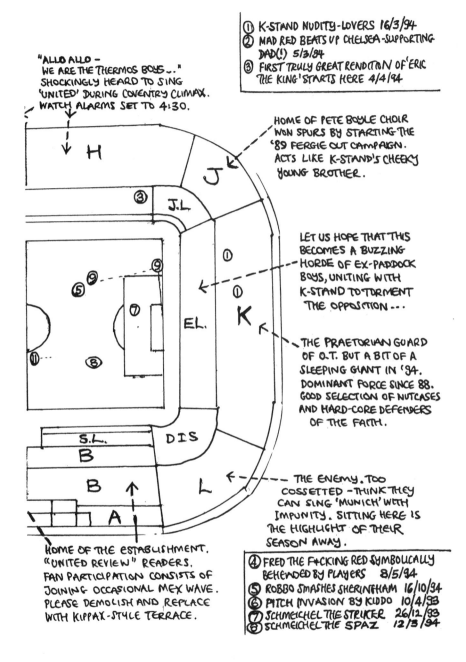

① K-STAND NUDITY-LOVERS 16/3/94
② MAD RED BEATS UP CHELSEA-SUPPORTING DAD(!) 5/3/94
③ FIRST TRULY GREAT RENDITION OF 'ERIC THE KING' STARTS HERE 4/4/94

"ALLO ALLO -
WE ARE THE THERMOS BOYS..."
SHOCKINGLY HEARD TO SING
'UNITED' DURING COVENTRY CLIMAX.
WATCH ALARMS SET TO 4:30.

HOME OF PETE BOYLE CHOIR
WON SPURS BY STARTING THE
'89 FERGIE OUT CAMPAIGN.
ACTS LIKE K-STAND'S CHEEKY
YOUNG BROTHER.

LET US HOPE THAT THIS
BECOMES A BUZZING
HORDE OF EX-PADDOCK
BOYS, UNITING WITH
K-STAND TO TORMENT
THE OPPOSITION...

THE PRAETORIAN GUARD
OF O.T. BUT A BIT OF A
SLEEPING GIANT IN '94.
DOMINANT FORCE SINCE 88.
GOOD SELECTION OF NUTCASES
AND HARD-CORE DEFENDERS
OF THE FAITH.

THE ENEMY. TOO
COSSETTED - THINK THEY
CAN SING 'MUNICH' WITH
IMPUNITY. SITTING HERE IS
THE HIGHLIGHT OF THEIR
SEASON AWAY.

HOME OF THE ESTABLISHMENT.
"UNITED REVIEW" READERS.
FAN PARTICIPATION CONSISTS OF
JOINING OCCASIONAL MEX WAVE.
PLEASE DEMOLISH AND REPLACE
WITH KIPPAX-STYLE TERRACE.

④ FRED THE F*CKING RED SYMBOLICALLY BEHEADED BY PLAYERS 8/5/94
⑤ ROBBO SMASHES SHERINGHAM 16/10/94
⑥ PITCH INVASION BY KIDDO 10/4/93
⑦ SCHMEICHEL THE STRIKER 26/12/93
⑧ SCHMEICHEL THE SPAZ 12/3/94

the victims of that particular scenario, Eric adding to his collection of absurdly fantastic goals in the latter.

The very best was reserved for away games; home sides forced to venture forward by capacity crowds played straight into the hands of United's gunslingers who were quite happy to sit back casually before bursting forward in cavalry charges to destroy terrified defences. At Hillsboro, The Dell, Bramhall Lane and Boundary Park, United were simply awesome, dishing out lessons in magisterial class that sent the home support away in humiliation. Even when we were not on song, victory still seemed inevitable, often achieved with the sort of touches that suggest divine support – Sharpe's outrageous volley at Goodison and Giggsy's one-two with the corner flag to set up the Highfield winner being perfect examples.

The peaks were surely at Villa Park and Maine Road. Forget the BBC's gushing guff about the Anfield game – that night in Birmingham marked the Premiership match of the season, featuring passing, movement and skill on a plane far above that inhabited by the rest of the League's mere mortals. (Pity about JD's mate getting arrested for buying a meat pie before half-time, though...West Midlands police have only become such knobs through years of practice you know.)

At City, their terrace humourists cleaned Moss Side out of Turkish Delight to celebrate our inglorious expedition to the land of corrupt, bum-molesting savages (that's Turkey, not Merseyside for once). Two down at half-time, predictable renditions of "Two nil up and you f*cked it up" floated over from their side of the Kippax sewer. That 15 minutes constituted the lowest point of our emotional season; a Leeds-style collapse hove appallingly into our view. Forty-five minutes of Cantona-inspired dominance later, Keane thrust the winner into the net, virtually combusted with delight and turned to marvel at the bedlam in our section of the stands. "Two nil up and you f*cked it up – City, City" filled the ghetto air – have the Bluenoses ever looked more suicidal than they did at that moment? United in general, and Eric in particular, had answered every post-Turkey question in the most emphatic fashion possible – the Red Army was back on the road to glory.

If we were going to be halted in our tracks, it appeared that the Christmas/New Year period would be the golden chance for our rivals to head us off at the pass. Three fixtures against our nearest challengers Villa, Newcastle and Blackburn, then a double-header against the twin forces of scum, Liverpool and Leeds. Each, apart from Leeds, raised their game for what were in effect their own Cup Finals, straining their second-rate sinews but failing to beat us – we emerged from the trial of strength unbroken. Leeds simply bottled out, their team's performance as abject as their fans', the clearest demonstration yet that they could no longer live with us. Two chants of "we are Leeds" and a microsecond of the airplane song – what mighty vocal support...

We rolled easily through January, stepping out on to the FA Cup trail with revenge at Bramhall Lane that featured a superb goal and a good Blade-kicking from Hughes; a comfortable win at Spurs followed. And then we ground to a shattering halt. Sir Matt Busby left us.

* * * * *

RED-EYE

"It was the 22nd January 1994, the first match after the tragic death of Sir Matt Busby. Everton were the opponents and their supporters had the good human decency to respect the minute silence which was moronically disrupted at other grounds around the country. The match was full of emotion and passion and played in the way appreciated by Sir Matt. The final whistle went and we had won one-nil. I was sitting in the old Stretford End near the tunnel and I stayed to clap the players in. 'We Are the Champions' was played over the tannoy and I held my scarf above my head and sang my heart out. Whilst I was doing so, Mark Hughes approached the tunnel. He looked up at me and eye contact was made; he held up the badge on his shirt and pointed at it while still looking at me as if to say, 'we're all part of this great club and it's something to feel proud of'. I lowered my scarf and glanced down at the club emblem on my shirt, looking back up I smiled and stuck my thumb up while nodding at him in agreement. He gave me the thumbs up, winked and then disappeared down the tunnel. This exchange took place within a few seconds and to me it epitomises the pride and passion felt by every true United supporter and United player at being part of the world's greatest football club, Manchester United.

"Brownie", Wellingborough

* * * * *

Only the most naive could have believed that the nationwide minute silences were going to pass peacefully. It was a mistake of the football establishment to claim Matt as some sort of national icon; we should have been left to celebrate his life by ourselves. Still, the call to silence did serve one useful purpose in highlighting to a nation at large which supporters had not yet evolved to the level of the rest. Step forward City, Sheff Utd, Chelsea and above all, Leeds. For Bittermen, you just have to feel disappointed. After all, Matt was once one of theirs; you would think that fellow Mancunians would be able to muster as much human decency as did the Scousers, to their credit.

Sadly it appears that a generation of bitterness and envy has distorted the genetics in the Blue corner of Manc – they seem to be breeding a special sort of grotesque creature there now that has more in common with the Leeds scum than other Mancs. Frankly, isn't it time we asked ourselves if this type of Bitter can be counted as a Manc any more, seeing as they lead the lifestyles of Scousers and exhibit the morality of the Scum. Is this the example of Manc-ness we want displayed to the world?

Leeds, however, took the media attention by disrupting the remembrance at Ewood Park live on Sky TV, to the disgust of Blackburn fans and all the players. They took the mother of all beatings from the tabloids as a result. All the Tykes had managed to achieve, apart from further sullying Revie's already tarnished memory, was to remind the nation (lest they forget past misdeeds) that many Leeds supporters remain the most provincial, ignorant, retarded and embarrassing collection of village idiots in football.

One of the sad aspects of the Leeds fan is that, remarkably, he will probably think he's quite a dude. Leeds-dwellers like to imagine themselves as the urban sophisticates of East of the Pennines, inhabiting a mighty imperial city. Pathetically, this 'huge conurbation', which can only support one barely successful football team that's spent most of its life in Division Two, is actually no more than an eye-sore of a shopping centre in the middle of the countryside with a few slums thrown in to contain the lowlife. In reality, it's about as urban as a cowpat – in Leeds, you're never more than five minutes away from a willing local sheep.

The Tykes love their rural mating-grounds; perhaps it reminds them of their roots from which they've only just evolved viz. the cave-dwelling Neanderthal that hunts dark-skinned animals and shags anything with an aperture. See, it sounds familiar doesn't it? Even the favourite Leeds song – 'United (Leeds) United (Leeds)' – with its deep-bass growl of the word 'Leeds' sounds like something from the soundtrack of a '50s dinosaur versus primitives movie. Once, having met a Leeds fan who exhibited human characteristics and could even talk in intelligible sentences, I asked him what this chant was supposed to achieve. "It's like in the film Zulu" he enthused, "it's like a native war cry to terrify the opposition." Sadly, he was quite serious. Ironically, in the film the Zulus, despite outnumbering the Brits 50 to 1, retreated; Michael Caine and company were dressed in red, white and black – another familiar scenario...

Leeds, in short, is *The Land that Time Forgot*. Throughout the '80s, it remained the Capital of Goth, populated by cretinous creatures obsessed by the Bauhaus and Banshees, loping through the streets in back-combed barnets and skin-tight black keks, the laughing stock of the nation's youth culture. In keeping with the city's spirit, the football fans continued to labour under the illusion that skinhead crops, Nazi ideology and mass violent disorder are still a groovy part of '90s terrace culture and that in the post-Hillsboro climate it might still be legitimate to make light of others' real life tragedies. The poor Tykes are stuck in a 1975-timewarp, deluded into believing their team are 'Champions of Europe', holding firm to the '70s hoolie philosophy of outrage and terror and unaware that the rest of the country has decided that Don Revie was a money-grabbing traitorous failure.

The one consolation for the rest of us is that although they are as obsessed as the Dirties and the Bitters about their public image and its perception by others, they are too stupid to work out the consequences of their actions. Even the most moronic of them must regret Ewood '94 – any sharp Scouser could have spotted the PR implications – but they just couldn't help themselves could they? You can take a Tyke out of the jungle but you can't take the jungle out of the Tyke.

* * * * *

The Busby disruptions were the most blatant symbol yet of the latest flesh-eating disease to sweep the nation – *rubrophobia virulens*, or manic Red-hating. Formerly confined largely to easily infested areas such as Murkeydive, Moss Side and Leeds where the local pond-life and general filth make any disease a good home, this United-loathing pestilence now seemed to be embedding itself under the skin of the nation at large, our on-field superiority and off-field 'arrogance' gnawing at the nerves of every outsider. Increasingly, opposing fans began to regress to the 1970s, treating Red visitors as invading warriors; with burning hostility, they sought to get their retaliation in first. (Awaydays were already troublesome enough as it was, thanks to the ticket priority given to exec and club class types – have the touts ever had a more profitable season?)

There had already been the customary skirmishing in Liverpool, producing the memorable sight of a large black Red personally 'addressing' a gathering of klansmen in the

152

Goodison stands. But now you could even count on a rabid reception at bumpkin outposts like Swindon and Blackburn, the latter occasioning running battles throughout the town afterwards. Perhaps more predictably, the Gooners and Hammers also tried their luck, West Ham resorting to other missiles when they ran out of bananas.

Unfortunately, Reds had probably sent out the wrong signals against Sheffield Wednesday in the boring home Coca semi. Owls fans had slyly attempted to allude to Munich, dressing it up as one of their own UEFA Cup-inspired rituals; the press bought this explanation but Reds at their end did not. A couple of hundred enraged United fans stepped outside to express their displeasure after the game and some regrettable scenes ensued. Most Reds refused to condone this but there was an underlying sense that at least other away fans' cards had been marked; just because our stewards and police were pathetically appeasing, that did not give visitors the right to pick at our wounds without fear of retribution.

In the return leg, United punished Trevor Francis' cocky presumption that Sheffield could overturn a one goal deficit by thrashing them 4-1. However, the hundreds of Wednesdayites who streamed out before full-time did so not only out of disgust but in preparation to wreak revenge for the OT scrummaging. By all accounts, those Reds who found themselves under attack aquitted themselves respectably.

There was no doubting that United were by now the most hated club in Britain – that, of course, is the corollary of being the most loved as well. There were two good reasons for this, apart from being Champions of course. Firstly, the fact that we have supporters in every town in Britain serves only to further antagonise the local team supporters as they are a daily in-yer-face reminder of the locals' inferiority. Secondly, the media attention that United get, which is above and beyond that afforded to past champions, must be pretty aggravating for those desperate to escape the glorification of our brilliant exploits.

Wherever you looked, whether it be in the papers, the footie mags, the style journals, the TV, the ad billboards, there were Champions United, dancing on the grave of rival teams' seasons. Your heart bleeds for them doesn't it? Naturally, the media allow themselves to be dominated by United because they're in the business of selling themselves and know that we are by far the best supported team – ergo the more good United news, the more sales. However, we were soon to discover the dark side of that equation – that more people hate United than any other club and that when there's bad tidings to be spread about us, it pays to smear them as widely and as melodramatically as possible. The Ides of March approached and the press would be determined to make the very most of them.

It might sound as perverse as a Leeds fan to say so but in retrospect, I'm glad we went through that agony in March and April. Frankly, the season was rolling by far too easily and that is not the United way of doing things. We'd reached the League Cup Final with our reserves and without breaking sweat; we'd cruised into the last eight of the FA Cup with televised demolitions of Norwich and Wimbledon, the Selhurst exhibition being particularly awesome; we were still well clear at the top after the thrilling win at QPR, although we could hear Blackburn's hooves in the distance behind us.

Surely we were not going to be allowed to float to the treble unmolested, without facing any adversity or crisis, without someone making us fight for it in hand-to-hand combat? Easy wins might have been acceptable at '80s Anfield but at OT, didn't we relish the backs-to-the-wall, drama-ridden, from-jaws-of-defeat stuff too much to be happy with a runaway title or Cup? Perhaps this is what a certain zine editor meant when I bumped into him on the Warwick Road – "I'm bleedin' bored" he complained, this just before the Chelsea match kick-off. Whatever heartache you went through over the next few weeks, you certainly couldn't claim it was boring.

Taking the Ides of March analogy, Julius Ceasar was obviously Eric, the Emperor of Old Trafford; the knife-wielding

Brutus was a certain green-robed git and the cowardly Senate who roared him on were the assembled whoring pigs of the tabloid press and TV studio couches. We should have known what to expect from these tat-peddlers from the start. Our fabulous, furious second-half display against Charlton was all but ignored as the media splashed Peter's moment of brain-death to the exclusion of all else, thus exhibiting the sense of proportion that has made our tabloids the envy of the world – not.

Johnny Giles then took it upon himself to lead a Cantona-backlash, the 'Man the Pros Read' producing the 'Column the Fans Piss On'. Eric promptly buried the sad, old Busby-reject by inspiring a night of magic against Wednesday. In the furore that was to come, that performance was so easily forgotten by the rest of the world, but not by us. A mad, wondrous evening – four top goals in one spell, a Hughes spectacular, a snow-storm, K-Stand's Barmy Army stripping off, Wednesday for-lornly singing "We want one" after our fifth goal...this coldest of nights had provided the warmest of memories.

And then the descent into the inferno. Four dropped points in the south was story enough for the closet-Scousers in the media, as Blackburn stormed up on the rails but the double sending-off of Eric wasn't just an excuse for a story – this was the cue for an orgy of anti-French racism in particular and anti-Red prejudice in general.

The fact that Vic Callow, in a bid to be a USA '94 ref perhaps, had made an horrendous cock-up at Highbury and that, therefore, only the stamping at Swindon was worthy of such hysteria wasn't going to stop the hack onslaught. By dredging up Eric's *faux pas* at Norwich, Peter's dismissal and even Sparky's at Sheffield, the media could add these to Eric's double and – hey presto – you've produced a 'Discipline Crisis at OT/Are United Going Off The Rails?' page-filler. Now, Keane and Ince, for months rightly portrayed as steely battlers, could be roped in for analysis and labelled mouthy neo-psychos, taking their place alongside the anti-Christ Cantona and the paranoid schizo Fergie.

Sadly, the fact that this was all fishy cobblers of the highest order, produced by barely-literate drunkards of no fixed principle, didn't stop it taking effect. In concrete consequence, this meant Eric being banned for five games at the most vital point of the season; the less tangible, but nevertheless apparent, further result was that the team as a whole were temporarily derailed, clearly feeling the pressure. Naturally, the next stage in the media campaign was to start talk of 'bottling it' whilst hyping-up Blackburn's chances of overhauling us. If Jack Walker had been paying the hacks himself, they couldn't have played it better.

* * * * *

In the five games that constituted the 'crisis weeks' that started and ended at Wembley, we came as close as you can to blowing all three legs of the treble that had until recently seemed ours for the taking. Thankfully, the only leg we actually lost was the one we scarcely cared about, Ron outsmarting Fergie yet again with a 4-1-4-1 formation manned by players who *needed* victory more than us. Eric, surrounded by markers, looked as miserable as we felt; the sending off of Andrei was a wretchedly cruel end to a day whose only bright spots had been the performance of the Pete Boyle Chorus at the Torch and the *News of the Screws*' story on 'Martin and delicious Debbie'.

Ewood Park sank us lower still; for once the execs had taken up all their tickets, leaving us bereft of vocal support, allowing the Scouse-swelled ranks to cheer The Greedy Bastards to victory. The mercenaries spent the next three weeks crowing, under the delusion that beating a Cantona-less United actually signified something. They might ruefully reflect now that they should've learned from Villa's mistakes in '93 – don't go taunting us about 'bottle' and claiming you're going to be champs until you're sure you've done the business. Still, what can you expect from such *nouveau riche* arrivistes who've had

156

no experience of the title game? Such mouthing off only displays a total lack of class – true thoroughbreds like United keep the trap shut and let the feet talk.

We showed our mettle against Liverpool and Oldham, prepared to slug it out spiritedly even though our inspiration had temporarily deserted us. The Scousers no doubt relished the prospect of halting a United title challenge again, although their 'witty' renditions of "Shearer" and "Blackburn" and the waving of red cards only served to prove that their own team's efforts had long since ceased to be worth shouting about. How sweet it was to hear Ronnie Moran "choking back the vomit" over the ref's no-penalty decision – now he knows what it was like for visitors to Anfield for a decade. Mind you, since this was the man who said after the 3-1 massacre in '89 "the best team lost", why does anyone pay any attention to his post-match comments anyway?

The Oldham match, psychologically at least, was crucial. An immediate bounce-back from Ewood was absolutely necessary, especially as they were our Cup semi opponents six days later. How ironic that the match-turning moment in the absence of Eric was to be provided by the man he replaced, Dion Dublin. So still we clung to that League lead we'd held since the beginning; Blackburn were still going to have to out-perform us and events were to demonstrate that they simply didn't have the bottle to pull it off. "Who the f*ck are Man United?" they would sing – and we shoved the answer down their throats.

The FA Cup Semi-Final at Wembley, April 10th: we were there under protest, forced to traipse down at Oldham's command because United refused to pull their weight and have it played up north. Edwards' PR gesture on coach prices only made it worse since the Club had announced the new kit details the same day, so pardon us for being cynical about the motives. Three players suspended, all of whom had been at their peak before the Ides, was handicap enough; add to that the missing hundreds of hard-core Reds who were unwilling

157

or unable to play the FA Wembley game and you have the recipe for season-slaying disaster.

For two hours, the football was the worst we'd seen for months, the atmosphere awful and the situation dire – a stupid, needless goal behind. Sometimes you watch United when they're trailing in the dying minutes and you still feel they can escape; the support reaches a crescendo and you live on, gripped by hope, until the whistle. But at that moment, I doubt whether many truly thought there was any chance of a reprieve. The entire afternoon and the whole situation had defeat written all over it. It just felt like the season was over and the players appeared to be just as resigned. It was a prolonged but inevitable death – you don't have hope as such, just a prayer for a miracle lodged with God.

The miracle came to pass. Somehow Hughes executed a volley of tremendous technique and power to score right in front of us with 40 seconds to go. For many of us, engulfed in the pandemonium that followed, that was the single most intense moment we'd ever had watching United. Unearthly sounds emitted from the throats of those around me, noises of ecstatic abandoned relief and joy that came from the some-where in the soul, not the larynx. Faces were contorted in paroxysms that I'd only seen before on warning films about rabies. Forget hindsight – surely everyone there *knew* that Hughes had saved not only the game but the season. You could see it in the expressions of everyone, of the delirious fans streaming out and of the players and the officials. The yawning abyss into which we'd been about to plunge disappeared at the second the ball crossed the line.

They say that after a near-death experience, life is twice as sweet and so it proved to be. Even when we cocked it up as at Wimbledon, it didn't actually matter because Blackburn had lost too. The rest of the run-in became a delight, a Triumph with Caesar Cantona back to lead his cohorts, our beaten rivals in chains behind us. The replay meant an extra match but it also entailed re-arranging the trip to Elland Road until after Eric's return – it couldn't have worked out better.

What is it about Maine Road semis and Man United? Every single one in living memory has produced a classic, full of vivid memories that never fade. The '94 replay was to be no exception. The jubilation of that night is now recalled with some poignancy, for it surely marked the last full-scale gathering of the Red Army infantry. Thousands packed into the condemned slum that is the Kippax, arms pinned to the sides in the closest non-homo camaraderie possible and roared through the OT songbook as Pete Boyle, poised precariously on someone's shoulders, attempted to cue us in for the season's hit, 'Eric the King'.

An old geezer next to me, struggling to keep conscious from the look of him, gasped happily "This is how it should be at every game" and who would disagree? It was hugely uncomfortable, the view was appalling, you couldn't even light your cig and the floor was covered in piss – just how we like it. Whilst we recreated the spirit of the Strettie, we sweated like bollocks. On the pitch too, testicles played a crucial role; Robbo scored with his scrotum, then Giggs later played a one-two off Pointon's ball-bag before scoring.

Andrei, though, was the true star. Once upon a time, he would set off on his gallops, only to meander manically around the pitch like an exploding space shuttle; now he had become the on-pitch personification of a Cruise missile, swerving beautifully around obstacles before homing in with deadly accuracy. His goal that night perfectly encapsulated his dazzling performance – the Kippax resounded to the clarion call "Andrei Must Say". Half of Oldham's fans hadn't bothered to turn up and those that did were as outclassed on the terraces as their team was on the pitch. The Double, which had recently seemed lost, was the odds-on target once more.

After the Wimbledon hiatus, we found ourselves presented with the most mouth-watering opportunity yet – the chance virtually to wrap up the trophy in four days by beating two of

our most loathed opponents, City and Leeds, the two sets of
supporters who'd disgraced themselves and outraged us back
in February. Eric was back, we were already at Wembley and
were firmly in pole position for the title sprint – the buzz around
OT was simply sensational. Bluenoses, having spent months
whinging about OT ticket allocations, ended up with a bonus
of half the Paddock but by half-time must have wished they
hadn't bothered.

Eric illuminated his come-back with two goals to silence the
assembled Magoos. Terry Phelan's threat to do his pitbull
impression for Eric failed to materialise as the World Cup loser
was left out. We'd secured the first Manchester League double
since 1979 and to that there was no answer from the Bittermen. Has there ever been such a massive disparity in class and
form between the two Manc sides in modern times? City have
now become so irredeemably second-rate that we barely count
them as rivals anymore – fanzine surveys demonstrate that
hatred of Leeds and 'Pool far outstrips the mild distaste and
feelings of pity we have for our Blue brethren.

Elland Road became the Last Chance Saloon for every
Red-hater in the land. Only a United defeat here could really
halt our march and what better candidates than Leeds to
attempt it? For months, the match had been relentlessly
hyped-up by the club and the Yorkshire media; the prospect
was even used as an inducement for fans to buy mini-season
tickets as the sad Tykes struggled to fill their new stand. The
home hordes were an extraordinary spectacle, proving that all
those who claim only a minority are infected by a venomous
Manc-hating are ignorant fools.

Their display of mass hostile hysteria, their exhibition of
uniform grunting, growling aggression and the widespread
assaults on United celebrators in the stadium gave the lie to
the Leeds PR image of a cleaned-up club supported by decent
Yorkie yeoman. Events outside the stadium convinced any
remaining doubters as mobs attacked both team and fan
coaches, waylaid family-type supporters and attacked the

police who had belatedly intervened. Fifty arrests, almost all Leeds, and 12 hospitalisations resulted; the police chief gave the habitual piss-poor self-justification for which, in an ideal world, he should have been sacked. The team provided the appropriate punishment for their animalistic antics, outclassing Leeds to win 2-0, with Hughes outstanding. Thirteen and a half years had now passed since Leeds last beat us, a run of abject failure that they richly deserve.

Coming from behind at Portman Road to win 2-1, after which the home fans came over to salute us, turned out to be the title-winning match. Blackburn couldn't take the pressure and lost their grip at Highfield Road, playing like pansies to be out-run by mid-table trundlers. Spookily enough, we had won the title on the same day as we had in '93, in the same circumstances – watching a Midlands game live on Sky won by a goal from a Liverpool fan. (Book now for Coventry away on April 29th – it could be the clincher!) The last two games became the celebratory highlights of a week-long party, tinged with regret as the Paddock held the last ever standing Old Trafford fans – United We Stood.

*　*　*　*　*

And so to Wembley, the final steps on the 20-year journey from relegation to the Double. You didn't have to be a G-Stand grumbling pensioner to feel that we had a historical wrong to right on May 14th; The Busby Babes had been robbed in 1957 thanks to McParland's assault on goalie Wood which, had it happened in modern times, could justifiably have led to criminal charges. We'd had the scent in our nostrils again in 1965 and 1976 but fallen at the last; in '83 and '85, we'd had to settle for the glory of Wembley alone as Scousers clinched the titles. Now, at last, the greatest United side for 30 years had the domestic game's greatest garland in their grasp. It was always an annoying anomaly that the name of Britain's biggest club was absent from the roll of Double honour; now only Chelsea stood in our way.

In the run-up to the Final, the Southern media frantically hyped up the Blues' chances, largely based on the wholly spurious grounds that they'd done the League double over us. This was supposed to demonstrate the cosmic power of the Chelsea God Squad, Messrs Hoddle and Peacock; The Chinned Wonder had the perfect tactical plans to beat the Reds which would be spear-headed by the Iraqi lookalike at Number 8. Of course, all Reds knew that Chelsea's League flukes had been entirely due to the absences of Hughes and then Eric; never in the past 20 years had the Red Army marched down to Wembley in such a spirit of overwhelming self-confidence. (Note for Bitter readers: 'Wembley' is the big place where good teams go to try and win silver cups – ask your Dad to explain.)

In a last thrust of psychological warfare, Hoddle proclaimed that he'd 'had a dream sent by God' in which he saw Chelsea beating Barnet before going on to Wembley victory – presumably an attempt to whip up some 'name-is-on-the-cup' belief in the Blue camp. After all, surely he could not be serious? If the leader of a modern organisation starts to babble about messages from Heaven – what is known in Manc as 'doing an Anderton' – isn't he to be metaphorically dumped in concrete at the first opportunity? Hey ho. Glenn succeeded only in making a complete arse of himself. His team of non-performing dwarves were duly crucified. Either God doesn't exist after all – and Hoddle needs to see a good shrink – or else He's got a bastard sense of humour. The Red Devils beat the Blue Evangelists as the heavens poured forth and the Double was done.

Granted, the match as a whole was no classic but the 10-minute spell after the hour was devastation defined; in the stands we were left panting and breathless, dizzy with elation, as one would expect after three climaxes in nine minutes. At 4:24pm, the first full-throated cry of "We've done the Double – tonight' resounded around the stadium, lyrically interchanging happily with 'shit on Chelsea....' to the same gleeful tune.

162

Chelsea, who'd spent the first half telling us they 'were back', sat transfixed with horror as they realised just what they'd come back to – getting obliterated by the Pride of the North in front of half a billion TV viewers.

Later, there was much talk of feeling sorry for plucky, unlucky Chelsea. To anyone at the sharp end of the Chelsea-United interface – i.e. anyone near K-turnstile – this would sound rather hollow.

Thanks to the usual farcical ticket allocation, huge swathes of the stands were totally mixed. As Eric slotted home number one, Chelsea fans in the corner showed their true colours by turning in packs on isolated Reds and laying into them. A rumble in the bars below soon followed and the last 10 minutes were filled with talk of post-match 'kick offs'. For a while, a re-run of September '77 seemed to be on the cards but in the event most Blues sloped off in humiliation after Incey and Choccy extracted the final drops of urine.

True enough, the numbers of arrests and injuries were the highest for a Cup Final in years but most observers agreed that it would have been much worse had the game finished only 2-0. Perhaps Chelsea fans can take comfort from the fact that their thrashing *on* the pitch saved them from a hiding off it; as it was, the only full-scale scrap took place in the tube station when a force of largely older Reds – K-standers perhaps – sorted out a Chelsea collection who'd been harrassing everyone in the vicinity. Spare any pity you have for Chelsea. They behaved crassly all day and got their just rewards. Just spare a thought for the good Burghers of Europe next season who'll have the dubious pleasure of receiving The Shed as visitors this year.

Still, not even the Stamford savages could spoil a magical day for Manchester United in which the Reds fulfilled a historic mission. Just as in Rotterdam, the euphoria was soaked in the Manchester rain we'd brought with us – it didn't matter since we were all to be internally soaked with Boddies for the next week or so. You could easily spot those who'd been to Wembley at the Hughesy Celtic game on Monday – they were the ones who'd reached the Keith Richards scale of utter wastedness. In just 34 days we had gone from the despair of being a minute away from defeat to Oldham – and the collapse of the entire season – to the Double Kings of England coronation. The media rent-a-quotes, taking their cue from an apoplectic Hansen, had tried to drum up a controversy about the second penalty 'turning point' but we all knew that we'd won the Cup the minute Denis Irwin blew up in the air as if he'd hit a mine – Eric would not miss and Chelsea would not come back from behind.

We may well be biased but that doesn't mean we can't speak the truth: United deserved to win the Double as no other team has done for at least 30 years. For the brilliance of so much of our game; for the character and resilience shown when all was against us; for the righting of history's wrongs; and for the magnificent devotion of us long-suffering fans – justice demanded that we did the Double. Now let's be the first to do it twice.

* * * * *

An Egyptian Tourism Minister, complaining about the problems caused by thousands of visitors to Cairo's antiquities, was asked by a hack if he appreciated the money such tourists were bringing into the Egyptian economy. "Of course I do," he replied "but can't they just send the cash and stay at home?" Such sentiments strike a chord with all hard-core Reds; the greatest drawback that's resulted from the media hype following May '93 has been the Invasion of the Day-Trippers at Old Trafford.

Stories about the part-timers' antics are legion, and by no means all apocryphal. Idiots troop up to *Red Ish* sellers and ask "Is that the prog.amme?"; families wander around outside Lou's chippy asking directions to the stadium; a group carrying so many loaded Superstore carrier bags got stuck in a main stand turnstile. No doubt such characters are heavy contributors to the OT Exchequer but at what cost? Who can be surprised about the declining strength of home vocal support when the stands are littered with extra-terrestrials who only know *We Are The Champions* and the ManU-Mag version of *We All Follow United*? Is there any sadder sound than the one I once heard in the North Lower – four face-painted teenage girls who, in between squeals of "Giggsy!" sang "If you are a City fan, surrender or you'll CRY?!?" It was a perfectly symbolic moment.

For too many, a trip to OT has become a sort of theme park experience for families, something to be appended to a list that already contains Alton Towers and Take That live. The Club have, of course, been all too eager to accommodate such aliens by creating an environment that is as safe, sterile and comfortable as an out-of-town DIY centre or multiplex, ready to welcome these new 'consumers' in hungry anticipation of the megadosh they'll shell out on the tacky merchandise and over-priced kits. Sometimes you hanker for a couple of Chelsea '77-style riots to frighten off such pondlife forever.

Naturally, the bottom line is the bottom line. Just as in the case of the execs, Club Class and the like, the worship by the club of 'the family' can always be justified by the accountants who run the Club in terms of income. In the short-term, they're right. If it's true that boxes alone bring in 25% of gate cash, then it's hard to dispute the rectitude of spending Development Association cash on such ventures. Pandering to the demands of the day-tripper may be distasteful but if it's paying Keano's wage bill, who can argue?

Similarly, our annual whinge about ticket price hikes is susceptible to criticism from the hard-line economist. An £11 minimum may seem a lot to us but if the laws of supply and demand were followed, we'd surely be facing prices of Chelseaesque proportions: if, say, 80,000 have applied for 15,000 match seats, you would have to reckon on a market-clearing price of at least £25 a throw. The harsh truth is that the Club could charge that amount every week and still fill the ground; surely the only reason they haven't done so is that Martin Edwards would not relish having 100,000 enraged Reds bearing down on his house waving pick-axes.

We are all, it seems, condemned to suffer the dictates of the money-Gods. However, the Club should beware of becoming enslaved to such short-termism. If you ignore the aspirations and the traditions of the true Red, if you continue to run the Club for the benefit of the families, the well-heeled and the part-timer, you run the risk of destroying the lifeblood of United. What happens if, God forbid, dark times return and nightmares fill the Theatre of Dreams? Will you still be able to count on 40,000 die-hards turning up every week to keep the Club afloat? If the teenagers and the less well-off have been driven out, do you think the fair-weather crowd will take up the slack?

Even now in these glorious times, the embourgeoisement of Old Trafford carries its own risks. Every time the PA is turned up to drown our prematch banter, every time lads are ejected for simply being boisterous and every time celebrators are hauled off to the nick for lighting a flare, you flatten the atmosphere a little further until, one day, there'll be nothing left. As Nick Hornby points out in *Fever Pitch*, do you imagine that the execs & co. come to OT just for the game? Of course not; they're there for the experience, the sense of occasion.

If OT were to become as lifeless as Ewood Park, they wouldn't turn up. And who is it who provides this sense of theatre? Us lot in the cheap seats, the ones who come for the football, not the day-trip and Superstore shopping, the ones who are being ignored, marginalised and forced out. You can't help feeling that the Club's ideal ground configuration would be a thousand exec boxes, an enormous family stand and the season ticket section; the rest of us are too much trouble – our 'unit-profit-ability' is too low for a PLC's liking. What they don't understand is that if WE weren't there, no one else would be either. In a sense, we are part of the *performance*, not the audience. The Club had better start looking ahead and treating us as an asset, not a liability because essentially *we* are Manchester United. Players come and go – we're here forever.

The Eric Cantona Interview

Bernard Morlino is a Parisian journalist who works for the weekly news magazine *Glode Hebdo*; he's also a Red fanatic who gets over to Old Trafford as often as work allows and drives around Paris blasting out recordings of the OT crowd that he's made on his visits to Manchester. In the spring, he did an interview with Eric The King, touching on Eric's views about the English, God, life and robots (!) – he was happy to let the first UK extracts appear in this volume. A fan since the heyday of Bobby Charlton, his own view of Eric and United is simple: 'How superb it is that Eric should find his home at such a sumptuous club as United.' Indeed.

BM: *Are the English more chauvinist than the French?*

EC: Yes, especially in football. In England, all things being equal, domestic players are preferred to foreigners. In France, it's the opposite.

BM: *According to you, what's the greatest difference between the French and English?*

EC: In England, one says 'it's done' whereas in France it's more a question of 'it's going to be done!' The more south you go, the more it rarely happens! The North is more disciplined. The French all give the impression of being a little more artistic and original. The English merge themselves a little more into the mould. We give the impression of knowing how to do everything whereas the English stay in their own role, conscious of their possibilities. That allows them to reach the elite in all domains and to better themselves without stepping anyone else's toes.

BM: *How does that translate itself in practice?*

EC: When a Frenchman shoots a film, he interferes in the scenario, the music, the décor – in short, he is everywhere! An Englishman surrounds himself with the best collaborators possible in order to make the best decisions. It's the right man in the right place. At Manchester United, I discuss money with an accountant and tactics with my manager, Alex Ferguson.

BM: *Why doesn't one see that in France?*

EC: Because in France, it's the press who make the teams. Apart from Platini and Guy Roux, the others simply go with the media flow. In France, the chairmen are there for their businesses and so that their businesses may continue to operate, they make sure the journalists are with them. The managers can't say anything in their own right! French chairmen help themselves from football whereas their English counterparts help football itself. When Ferguson said "I must have Cantona in my team", the chairman of United said OK. Then I arrived!

BM: *How does the English press behave with you?*

EC: Sometimes the press shadow me in search of scandal. The English are a little like the Americans of Europe, they have the same morals and their laws authorise the press to interfere in the private lives of celebrities. Here, they go on for ages about a star who cheats on his wife. Some journalists have already tailed me in my car. It's like a real spy movie! They've even tried to offer me a cigarette to make me appear debauched!

BM: *In France, you didn't get anything like that...*

EC: No, never! It's a pity that this type of behaviour has rubbed off on the English, who have very much got on their high moral horse. I was taken aside at a friend's house by a young 18-year old girl who said to me before I'd said a word: "What are you doing? You're married – you shouldn't be going out alone. You should be at home!"

BM: *What strikes you most about England?*

EC: Unemployment, as in France. A business manager cannot dispense with machines which cost less than workers. Moreover, machines don't go on strike. It's known that the more one creates machines the less place there is for workers. I have my own idea to combat the rise of robots and computers; there should be a law taxing machines as well as workers! Thus at last one would be able to choose between the two. Then the State would give back the money to the unemployed!

BM: *What do you think about royalty?*

EC: The guards, the horses and the protocol are at the same time beautiful and obsolescent. It shows respect and class to keep traditions; however, I'm not in favour of inherited privilege!

BM: *Do you ever think of converting to Protestantism?*

EC: If I HAD to choose, I would be Protestant. But deep down, I am an existentialist. I am born, I live and I die. To believe in life after death is a sort of weakness. Existentialism I learned first from Sartre and Camus and then I took the road alone. To '*I am, therefore I think*' I add '*I am not, therefore I do not think!*' When you're dead, you're dead, that's for sure. There'll be no Ouija boards; no one will be calling me!

BM: *Do you believe in God?*

EC: My religion is to give everything I have to give and, thereafter, if I am no longer anything at all, it's not serious. I only believe in what I can see, like Saint Thomas.

BM: *In coming here, what have you escaped from?*

EC: From the French football world, not France as such. I left my country because it doesn't love sport or sportsmen. In France, sport is treated like shit and sportsmen like illiterates.

France recognise the intelligence of the spirit but not that of the body.

BM: *And in England the sportsman is...*

EC: The sportsman is recognised like other people are. His is a sort of intellect that uses another kind of knowledge.

BM: *How do you prepare for matches?*

EC: I simply force myself to destroy all negative images. The match itself is all about anticipation. You need to know what your team mates and opponents are gong to do and position yourself on the pitch accordingly. A great team foresees every-thing, thanks to a complementary merging of action and spirit. A long, deep ball, a chase and a conclusion; it's pure spatial geometry.

BM: *How has football in England changed you?*

EC: I can say that I've rediscovered a joy in living and playing. The English aren't afraid of telling me that they love me. If I am sad, waves of other people haul me back towards the top. As soon as I cross the threshold of the dressing room, a whirlwind transports me. Around me all I see are good people. That's what get me going the best.

BM: *Are there rivalries between you?*

EC: Yes, but the English anticipate reactions in order to kill the chicken in the egg before it hatches(!). The day after I won the PFA Award, a player said 'since he was elected, he's let himself go'. Everyone laughed their heads off. In France, they get mired in psychodramas.

BM: *Why do the English appreciate you more than the French?*

EC: The French just took me to be a capricious child!

Quelques bon mots d'Eric:

"Everything is a question of roots. Manchester United lived before me and will live long after me."

"I want to die from an overdose of love."

"The man comes first, then the player."

"When I speak to a journalist, I empty myself as if I were before a psychoanalyst."

The Greatest Double of all Time?

No sooner had McClair side-footed the fourth at Wembley, the debate about the best double ever started. Predictably, the massed ranks of Scouse commentators claimed in unison that their '86 triumph was the zenith of world footie achievement. Do the stats bear this out?

As every schoolboy knows, before 1994 only five teams had won the League and Cup in the same season. We can dismiss Preston's 1889 side and Villa's 1897 team straight off; we are all aware that old football was rubbish and that at the time there were only about five teams in the entire country. The real contenders are Arsenal, Spurs, 'Pool and us.

League Title Records

1960/61	Spurs	PL42	W31	D4	L7	PTS66	78.6%
1970/71	Arse	PL42	W29	D7	L6	PTS65	77.4%
1985/86	Scouse	PL42	W26	D10	L6	PTS88	73.9%
1993/94	United	PL42	W27	D11	L4	PTS92	77.4%

What strikes you immediately is that Liverpool are the least impressive of all these Champion teams on playing record alone; United are level with The Arse and a sliver behind Spurs – more tellingly, we were the least-defeated team of all. Since being Champion is about invincibility, doesn't that count for most? Only THREE teams could beat us in the League, by far the best record on that issue. Let's take the issue of dominance further; who were the title rivals and by how much did the Champs beat them – and how good were the rival teams anyway.

1960/61	2nd Sheff Wed (58pts)	3rd Wolves (57)	Title Lead: 8 points
1970/71	2nd Leeds (64)	3rd Spurs (52)	Title Lead: 1 point
1985/86	2nd Everton (86)	3rd West Ham (84)	Title Lead: 2 points
1993/94	2nd Blackburn (84)	3rd Newcastle (77)	Title Lead: 8 points

Only Spurs and United can boast domineering leads over the also-rans; Arsenal and 'Pool squeezed in with one and two points to spare respectively. Indeed, both Arse and 'Pool didn't hit the top until the last few weeks of the season and neither had been favourites during the season whereas Spurs and United went straight to the top and remained there until the death – truly commanding performances. This is the nub of the matter; the fact is that the Champions of 1971 and 1986 could not really claim to be the best teams in Britain at the time, unlike Spurs and us.

As Alan Hansen admitted on Cup Final day, as late as March '86, he was telling Dalglish that Liverpool weren't good enough to top Everton. The Blues did the League double over 'Pool and outplayed them for 60 minutes in the Cup Final; Dalglish had said in March that 'Pool would do it if they "had some good luck" which is precisely what they got in spades full. The truth is that from 1984/85 to 1986/87, Everton were the best in the country – *they* deserved the Double in '86, not 'Pool. The most biased of Anfield-watchers freely admit that the 'Pool of 1985-87 wasn't as good as the sides of '84 or '88.

As for Arsenal, they won their title by default; Leeds, who *were* the best in Britain then, were robbed of the title by an outrageous refereeing decision. If proof were needed of Arsenal's lack of worthiness, consider this: the so-called great '71 team failed to win a single trophy afterwards. The Double was won out of the blue by a singularly undeserving team.

No, the truth is that only Spurs and United are in contention for the 'Greatest Double Team of all Time'. Both won the League by a mile, having led from the start; both were clearly recognised as not only the best teams in England but also as the purveyors of a brand of exciting football that most fans wished to see. No doubt, Spurs were a truly great side but one suspects that they are over-lauded by the game's Southerners, keen to put one of theirs above Northern greats in the pantheon of football.

Their playing record in '61 was slightly superior to ours and their lead over other teams slightly greater, admittedly. But United were the more invincible; almost a third of the Division could point to victories over the Champs at the end of the '61 campaign. Secondly, consider the rivals. Spurs outpaced Sheff Wed, who in '61 were making their ONLY post-war appearance in the top three – hardly a class act to beat.

Wolves, in third, were on the edge of an historic decline and never in the running. United, in contrast, faced young, hungry teams who would have made worthy champs in any other year and who surely will continue to challenge for honours in future seasons. So it was too in the Cup; United drawn away to Premier opposition in all but one case whereas Spurs had it easy – contrast the Finals where Spurs laboured to beat a poor, tired Leicester side in the worst Final of the '60s as against United's record-equalling hammering of a surprisingly good Chelsea team.

Finally, to clinch the argument, consider the wider picture. Spurs, supposedly the team of the century, only won that one title. Before '61 they'd been second best to both United in 1956/57 and Wolves in 1958/59. Sure, they won the FA Cup and ECW Cup after 1961 but United had already won those by 1994 – and of course, we've already won more titles than that Spurs team, with more to come alongside a European Cup we hope. The case is proved:

UNITED – *GREATEST DOUBLE WINNERS OF ALL-TIME!*

United's League Record 1986-1994

Season	PL	W	D	L	FOR-AG	PTS	5	POSN	Top scorer
1986/87	42	14	14	14	52-45	56	50.0	11th	Davenport 14
1987/88	40	23	12	5	71-38	81	72.5	2nd	McClair 24
1988/89	38	13	12	13	45-35	51	50.0	11th	Hughes 14
1989/90	38	13	9	16	46-47	48	46.1	13th	Hughes 13
1990/91	38	16	12	10	58-45	59	57.9%	6th	McClair, Bruce 13
1991/92	42	21	15	6	63-33	78	67.9%	2nd	McClair 18
1992/93	42	24	12	6	67-31	84	71.4	1st	Hughes 15
1993/94	42	27	11	4	80-38	92	77.4%	1st	Cantona 18
Total	322	151	97	74	482-312	62.0%			
Under Ferguson	309	148	93	68	466-296	62.9%			

Avge per season: Goals for 60, against 39; League position 6th.
Average 1975-94: Goals for 64, against 43; League position 5th, % 61.48

United's Overall 1st Class Record 1986-94

Season	PL	W	D	L	For-AG	%	Lge	FAC	FLC	EUR	CHS	Top scorer
1986/87	48	17	15	16	61-52	51.0	11th	rd4	rd3	"	—	Davenport 16
1987/88	48	29	12	7	86-40	72.9	2nd	rd5	QF	"	—	McClair 31
1988/89	48	18	15	15	62-41	53.1	11th	QF	rd3	"	—	McClair, Hughes 16
1989/90	49	20	12	17	64-61	53.1	13th	WON	rd3	"	—	Hughes 15
1990/91	60	32	16	12	101-63	66.7	6th	rd5	R-UP	WON	DRW	Hughes, McClair 21
1991/92	58	30	20	8	85-43	69.0	2nd	rd4	WON	rd2	ESC	McClair 24
1992/93	50	27	14	9	73-35	68.0	1st	rd5	rd3	rd1	—	Hughes 16
1993/94	63	42	14	7	125-56	77.8	1st	WON	R-UP	rd2	WON	Cantona 25
Total	424	215	118	91	657-391	64.6						
Under Ferguson	407	210	113	84	633-369	65.5						
Cups	102	64	21	17	175-79	73.0						
Under Ferguson	98	62	20	16	167-73	73.5						

United Champion Ratings 1992/3 & 1993/4

These average ratings for the players are calculated from an average of all the newspaper form marks; 100 is merely average, 150 is very good indeed and anything approaching 200 brilliant. That Incey and Eric can *average* near 200 just shows how fabulous those two players in particular have been since '92. NB: MOM means Man-of-the-Match awards.

1992/93

Player	Score	MOM
Cantona	196	4
Ince	187	8
Giggs	163	7
Hughes	162	5
Robson	153	-
Bruce	152	3
Schmeichel	142	5
Sharpe	138	2
Ferguson	137	1
Pallister	134	4
Irwin	127	2
Phelan	123	-
Dublin	117	1
Parker	116	1
McClair	112	3
Kanchelskis	100	-
Blackmore	88	-

1993/94

Player	Score	MOM
Ince	206	7
Cantona	180	10
Hughes	178	8
Kanchelskis	169	4
Giggs	167	1
Bruce	159	3
Keane	152	8
Pallister	147	4
Schmeichel	146	5
Sharpe	139	4
Parker	135	2
Irwin	133	1
Robson	122	1
Dublin	110	1
McClair	97	1
Phelan	97	-

The five top-rated performances in each season were:

1992/93

CANTONA at Norwich; CANTONA v Aston Villa; SHARPE v Chelsea; PALLISTER at Coventry; SCHMEICHEL at Leeds

1993/94

CANTONA v Aston Villa; CANTONA v Sheff Wed; INCE at Aston Villa; KANCHELSKIS v Oldham (semi); HUGHES at Leeds

The only other player to rate a 180 average in the last two seasons was David Batty at Blackburn last season. Reds rule as usual...

United v The Dirties – In Europe

In the Merseyside pubs I am forced to inhabit – sawdust on the floor, prozzies at the door – I often translate the vowel-strangling Scouse dialects to discover what the dustbin-dippers are thinking. Currently, they are all petrified that United will continue to emulate the fading glories of their '80s team by lifting at least one Euro Cup in the near future and are preparing their 'intellectual' defences. These seem to consist of arguing that until United win FOUR more Euro Cups, we will remain England Number Two in this respect. Whilst you can't fault the arithmetic, the reality is surely more complex. The fact is that the UEFA foreigner rule distorts any possible comparison. United set out with an enormous handicap; not only are we prevented from fielding our Champion side but, in effect, we are further prevented from signing any non-Anglo ever again. ANY English club attempting to win a modern Euro Cup faces a far sterner struggle than the 'easy' English winners of 1977-84.

Secondly, the new League structure of the tournament increases the task markedly. Teams cannot slime their way to the Final via soft clubs with a lucky draw – now you cannot escape facing all the best Euro outfits. Furthermore, teams face more games at a consistently higher level of opposition these days; no more first two rounds of Finnish or Cypriot no-hopers before you run into the big boys. I may be biased but as a footballing achievement, a '90s Euro Cup is going to be worth two of its predecessors in real terms. But apart from all this, what of the past? Were the Scouse wins achieved between '77 and '84 really so marvellous?

It must be a huge source of aggravation to the Scouse that the image of United's '68 Euro win is imprinted indelibly on the nation's consciousness whereas one struggles to summon up visions of Scouse in Europe beyond those from Heysel. With the possible exception of 1977, none of 'Pool's Euro Cups seemed to bring them the glory and glamour that ours did. How very sad for them. Why is this? Brian Glanville, Britain's top soccer writer, wrote a definitive history of the Euro Cup tournament and provides some useful reflections. Quite rightly, he lambasts the entire decade of the Euro Cup from 1978 onwards as being boring, negative and destructive; whilst admiring the achievements of England's victorious clubs, he deplores the methods used and the lack of style these clubs exhibited. What good had they done for English soccer at a deeper level? None at all.

There's nothing new in that perhaps. All United fans know from being forced to watch the Anfield Machine for so long that Liverpool were tedium personified; only in 1987/88 could any sane neutral have wished to pay money to watch them. Still, a Euro Cup's a Euro Cup, however you win it – it's just that if you do it the way the English did it during those years, it's not quite as glorious is it?

Glanville hints at another salient point when he quotes Bob Paisley after Forest ko'd 'Pool in 1978/79. Apparently, Paisley – with a typical lack of grace – had said Forest would easily win the Cup because there were no good teams any more on the Continent. When he was reminded of this observation after 'Pool's '81 win, he naturally reacted rather badly to this since such a viewpoint clearly devalued 'Pool's "glorious triumph". But the point is a valid one. Those years seemed bereft of Euro super-clubs; can you name the one great side from those times to compare with the Milan, Barca or Marseilles of the early '90s? Or with the giants of the '60s for that matter? Of course you can't, because there weren't any. Liverpool and the rest were competing in a virtual vacuum of Euro talent. These were the years when, on the Continent at least, national sides' pre-eminence over club sides was at its apex. This is how great national achievements such as Germany in 1980, Italy in '82 and France in '84 were wrought. Contrast this with the '90s and '60s when Euro football nations – Germany apart – were a uniformly poor bunch; the club sides were the dominant forces.

The facts bear out this impression. To win a Euro Cup in the '60s, a club would be faced with the mighty challenge posed by a host of Euro super-clubs, teams who won domestic titles with unerring regularity before proceeding unfailingly to semis and finals of the Euro Cup. Inter and AC Milan, Barca and Real and, of course, the brilliant Benfica – their names stuffed the semi-final placings of the '60s' tournaments. Similarly, in the '90s, the Cup is dominated by three or four superteams – there is simply no way to slime your way to a soft Euro Cup any more.

Not so in the barren years of 1977-85. In those nine seasons where English success was concentrated, a look at the teams who reached semi-finals is instructive. Who else apart from Liverpool was regularly reaching semis, thus proving themselves to be a mighty team? Amazingly, only Juventus managed to reach three semis – Forest and Inter Milan got to two. What a pathetic display! Every season, ridiculous minnows would sail through to the edge of the Final itself. Remember Austria WAC?! Dinamo Bucharest? Gotenburg?! Panatha-bloody-naikos?! All these non-entities made the semis in those years, much to the delight of Liverpool who managed to draw two of these themselves. For God's sake, a bunch of Swedish yak-farmers from Malmo actually made it to the Final. What glory is there in emerging as the best from such an motley crew?

A check on the title honours in Europe in those years reveals the lack of great dominant clubs who could've at least given Liverpool a run for their money. In those nine seasons, six different clubs won French titles; five in Germany; four in Spain and Italy. Real Madrid won a treble of titles but this was more a testament to Barca's decline than Real's worth – Glanville called them one of the worst Spanish Euro finalists ever. Only Juventus, who won four titles in this period, finally fit the super-club bill; as we know, when 'Pool finally met Juve in the tournament, Juve won. So it was a dodgy penalty given amidst the stench of death but is any Scouser going to argue that Juve, containing Tardelli, Rossi, Platini, Boniek and Cabrini, were not the greater side in the mid-'80s?

Does any of this matter? It clearly does to the Scouse, as witnessed by the preponderance of banners in the Kop that trumpet Liverpool's historical successes. One at the 3-3 thriller said: "Form is temporary – class is permanent." and listed 'Pool's Euro Cup wins underneath. If they think that winning four Euro Cups, three of them in the most boring manner imaginable, in an era when there was no competition is a sign of *class*, then so be it! The naked truth is that in Europe, as in Britain, Liverpool have had the greatest fortune of all – to be at their peak when no one else could consistently get their act together.

United Managers' Success Rates 1975-1994

Manager	All Games	League	Cups	Av.Lge.Gls
T. Docherty	64.4%	61.3%	74.1%	70-52
D. Sexton	56.3%	57.4%	50.0%	61-49
R. Atkinson	63.6%	62.6%	66.7%	67-38
A. Ferguson	65.5%	62.9%	73.5%	60-39

United Goalscorers' Strike Rates 1986-1994

Player	Games	Goals	Games per Goal
1. Cantona	71	34	2.09
2. Hughes	300	103	2.91
3. McClair	345	115	3.00
4. Whiteside	72	20	3.60
5. Davenport	95	26	3.65
6. Robins	68	17	4.00
7. Giggs	150	36	4.17
8. Stapleton	40	9	4.44
9. Wallace	70	11	6.36
10. Dublin	16	2	8.00

Records Under Fergie

Record Wins of 5-0 versus: Hull City, Sept 1987; Rotherham, Oct 1988; Luton, Sept 1991; Coventry, Dec 1992; Sheff Wed, March 1994.

Record Away Win: 6-2 at Arsenal, Nov 1990.

Record Defeats: away – City, 1-5, Sept 1989; home – QPR, 1-4, Jan 1992.

Worst League Run: 11 without a win, Nov '89-Feb '90. Also, 6 games without a Red scoring, Mar-Apr '89.

Best League Run: 22 without defeat, Sept '93-Mar '94 (in a run of 37 undefeated in all competitions).

Goalscoring: United scored 16 in four games in Dec '91.

Defending: United conceded only 3 in the first 14 games of '91/92.

United v The Bittermen, The Sheep and The Dirties, 1975/94

United v Liverpool

Season	(H)	(A)	(Cups)	
1975/76	0-0	1-3		
1976/77	0-0	0-1	2-1	
1977/78	2-0	1-3	0-0	
1978/79	0-3	0-2	2-2, 1-0	
1979/80	2-1	0-2		
1980/81	0-0	1-0		
1981/82	0-1	2-1		
1982/83	1-1	0-0	1-2	
1983/84	1-0	1-1	2-0	
1984/85	1-1	1-0	2-2	2-1
1985/86	1-1	1-1	1-2 (A)	
1986/87	1-0	1-0		
1987/88	1-1	3-3		
1988/89	3-1	0-1		
1989/90	1-2	0-0		
1990/91	1-1	0-4	3-1 (H), 1-1	
1991/92	0-0	0-2		
1992/93	2-2	2-1		
1993/94	1-0	3-3		

H:	PL20	W7	D10	L3	F21	A16
A:	PL20	W5	D6	L9	F18	A30
N:	PL9	W4	D4	L1	F13	A9
TOTAL:	PL49	W16	D20	L13	F52	A55

Success Rate: Man United 53.1%, Liverpool 46.9%

United v Man City

Season	(H)	(A)	(Cups)
1975/76	2-0	2-2	0-4(A)
1976/77	3-1	3-1	
1977/78	2-2	1-3	
1978/79	1-0	3-0	
1979/80	1-0	0-2	
1980/81	2-2	0-1	
1981/82	1-1	0-0	
1982/83	2-2	2-1	
1985/86	2-2	3-0	
1986/87	2-0	1-1	1-0(H)
1989/90	1-1	1-5	
1990/91	1-0	3-3	
1991/92	1-1	0-0	
1992/93	2-1	1-1	
1993/94	2-0	3-2	

H:	PL16	W9	D7	L0	F26	A13
A:	PL16	W5	D6	L5	F23	A26
TOTAL:	PL32	W14	D13	L5	F49	A39

Success Rate: United 64.1%, City 35.9%

United v Leeds

Season	(H)	(A)	(Cup)
1975/76	3-2	2-1	
1976/77	1-0	2-0	2-1
1977/78	0-1	1-1	
1978/79	4-1	3-2	
1979/80	1-1	0-2	
1980/81	0-1	0-0	
1981/82	1-0	0-0	
1990/91	1-1	0-0	2-1(H), 1-0(A)
1991/92	1-1	1-1	3-1(A), 1-0(A)
1992/93	2-0	0-0	
1993/94	0-0	2-0	

H:	PL12	W6	D4	L2	F14	A9
A:	PL14	W7	D6	L1	F16	A8
N:	PL1	W1	D0	L0	F2	A1
TOTAL:	PL27	W14	D10	L3	F32	A18

Success Rate: United 70.4%, Leeds 29.6%

◻ City haven't won at OT since we got promoted.

◻ It is now (summer 1994) 13½ years since Leeds last beat us.

◻ Assuming the Bitters cock it up again next Derby, they'll only have won ONE in the last 20. Still say that 5-1 wasn't a fluke?!

◻ In the big Wembley games and semis, the Scouse have only won once in NINE attempts – when United were down to 10 men.

◻ The savages at Elland Road have only seen their heroes score TWO goals against us in 14 years.

◻ In the entire 'Anfield Decade' of the 1980s, 'Pool could only beat us once in the League at their hovel.

◻ Our success rates since Sexton got sacked are even better:

United	56.1%	Scouse	43.9%
United	68.4%	Bitters	31.6%
United	75%	Scum	25%

WORRIED BY THOSE EXPENSIVE END OF SEASON TRIPS TO WEMBLEY?

All those rip-off prices and
the struggle to get tickets?
Overcome the problem simply
by supporting Manchester City.
We've won fuck all in 18 years.
NO CUP FINALS! NO TROPHIES! NO WORRIES!

(Leaflet sent around Manchester, April '94)

183

MACCLESFIELD: THOSE WERE THE DAYS – Doug Pickford *(£7.95)*
DARK TALES OF OLD CHESHIRE – Angela Conway *(£6.95)*
MAGIC, MYTH AND MEMORIES: The Peak District – Doug Pickford *(£7.95)*
MYTHS AND LEGENDS: East Cheshire and the Moorlands – Doug Pickford *(£7.95)*
SUPERNATURAL STOCKPORT – Martin Mills *(£5.95)*

Hill Walking for all!

CHALLENGING WALKS IN NORTH-WEST BRITAIN – Ron Astley *(£7.95)*
LAKELAND ROCKY RAMBLES: Geology beneath your feet – Brian Lynas *(£9.95)*
FIFTY CLASSIC WALKS IN THE PENNINES – Terry Marsh *(£8.95)*
RAMBLES IN NORTH WALES – Roger Redfern
HERITAGE WALKS IN THE PEAK DISTRICT – Clive Price
EAST CHESHIRE WALKS – Graham Beech
WEST CHESHIRE WALKS – Jen Darling
WEST PENNINE WALKS – Mike Cresswell
NEWARK AND SHERWOOD RAMBLES – Malcolm McKenzie *(£5.95)*
RAMBLES IN NORTH NOTTINGHAMSHIRE – Malcolm McKenzie
RAMBLES AROUND MANCHESTER – Mike Cresswell
WELSH WALKS: Dolgellau /Cambrian Coast – L. Main & M. Perrott *(£5.95)*
WELSH WALKS: Aberystwyth & District – L. Main & M. Perrott *(£5.95)*
PUB WALKS IN THE LAKE DISTRICT – Neil Coates

Even easy-peasy walks:
LAKELAND WALKING, ON THE LEVEL – Norman Buckley
MOSTLY DOWNHILL: LEISURELY WALKS, LAKE DISTRICT – Alan Pears
MOSTLY DOWNHILL: PEAK DISTRICT (White Peak) – Clive Price
MOSTLY DOWNHILL: PEAK DISTRICT (Dark Peak) – Clive Price
– all of these books are currently £6.95 each, except where indicated

And there's more ...

**A fabulous series of 'Pub Walks' books for just about every popular
walking area in the UK • A new series of investigations into the
Supernatural • popular computer books**

– plus many more entertaining and educational books being regularly added to
our list. All of our books are available from your local bookshop. In case of
difficulty, or to obtain our complete catalogue, please contact:

**Sigma Leisure, 1 South Oak Lane, Wilmslow, Cheshire SK9 6AR.
Phone: 01625 531035   Fax: 01625 536800**
ACCESS and VISA orders welcome – call our friendly sales staff or use our
24 hour Answerphone service! Most orders are despatched on the day we
receive your order – you could be enjoying our books in just a couple of days.